Concepts in geography
1 Settlement patterns

Concepts in geography

Concepts in geography

1 Settlement Patterns

J A Everson Head of Geography Department, City of London School

B P FitzGerald Head of Geography Department, St Dunstan's College

Longmans

Longmans, Green and Co Ltd
London and Harlow
Associated companies, branches and representatives throughout the world

© *Longmans, Green and Co. Ltd 1969*
First published 1969

Made and printed in Great Britain by
William Clowes and Sons, Limited, London and Beccles

Contents

Preface

The major changes in geography courses at many British and most American and Swedish universities have yet to be passed on to the schools. Teachers aware of changes are faced with a familiar dilemma; existing curricula tend to reflect a traditional view of the field which despite its intrinsic merit is increasingly at odds with current theory and practice at the university level. Curricula are supported by an interlocking system of textbooks, examinations, and training patterns so that any innovation within this strongly-structured system is likely to be slow and difficult.

This book by John Everson and Brian Fitzgerald represents an important step in loosening these constraints. It shows a fresh and novel approach to settlement geography which links familiar spatial patterns to newer methods of analysis and stresses the excitement of individual discovery. Its modular form suggests that it can be fitted into existing curricula with a minimum of disturbance, and yet it lays the basis for more wholesale change in the future.

It is now five years since the University of Cambridge Extra-Mural Board launched the Madingley Seminars in Geography in which university teachers and researchers tried to set out current changes in the field for practising teachers. It is particularly encouraging to see two of the original members of that course taking up the challenge thrown out then in such a vigorous and exciting way.

Peter Haggett
University of Bristol,
September 1968.

Acknowledgements

We are indebted to the following for permission to reproduce copyright material: Clarendon Press, Oxford for extracts from *The Open Fields* by C. Stewart Orwin and C. S. Orwin and Lund University, Sweden, for extracts from *Theoretical Geography* by W. Bunge (Lund University Studies series C), and to the following for permission to use copyright material in the preparation of figures: Edward Arnold (Publishers) Ltd for figs 64, 71 from Haggett, *Locational Analysis in Human Geography*; British Railways for figs 77, 78, 81; The English Universities Press Ltd for fig. 6 from Mitchell, *Historical Geography*; Geographical Publications Ltd for figs 15, 16, 17 from the *First Land Utilisation Survey*; University of Lund, Sweden, for fig. 52 from *Lund Studies in Geography*, Ser. B, No. 24, pp. 558–9; Oxford University Press for figs 25, 28, 29 from Orwin & Orwin, *Open Fields*; Sir Isaac Pitman & Sons Ltd for fig. 1 from Dury, *Map Interpretation*; *Sociological Review* for fig. 44 from article by McClelland, Vol. 10, 1962; the Ministry of Transport for fig. 83 and Yale University Press for fig. 70 from Lösch, *Economics of Location*. Figs 59, 60 are reprinted from Brian J. L. Berry, *Geography of Market Centers and Retail Distribution*, (C) 1967, by permission of Prentice-Hall, Inc., Englewood Cliffs, New Jersey and fig. 56 is reproduced from the Ordnance Survey Map with the sanction of the Controller, H.M. Stationery Office. Crown copyright reserved.

Introduction

Many changes in the scope of and approach to geography have been taking place in our universities within the last few years. Many of these changes are slowly penetrating school geography in a piecemeal and uncoordinated fashion. Teachers are beginning to realise that much of what is taught in our schools is purely repetitive and lacks intellectual stimulus and challenge to the student. Basic to these changes, we feel, is an ability on the part of the student to appreciate fundamental concepts in geography: those concerned with space, location, and interactions through time.

We strongly refute the viewpoint that sixth-form geography is encroaching on the universities' work. That is to imply that a concept can only be taught at one level or only once. In the past Central Place Theory has been one of the ideas generally taught in the universities and thought to be too complex for school study. However, this and other basic concepts can be introduced early in the school geography syllabus and then developed further as the student progresses through the school. J. S. Bruner has said in *The Process of Education* (New York, Vintage Books, 1960): 'A curriculum as it develops should revisit these basic ideas repeatedly, building upon them until the student has grasped the full formal apparatus that goes with them.' This then, is the 'spiral curriculum' which, if adopted, would give a much needed structure to the subject in our schools.

In response to such changes we have written these first two books on aspects of settlement geography. An understanding of urban geography seems essential for members of already large and still growing urban communities. In the first volume rural settlement and the influence towns have on each other and on their surrounding regions are discussed, while the second deals with the growth and internal differentiation of the town itself.

We have selected in each book those concepts which appear to us to be the most important in this field. The student is encouraged to learn through discovering them for himself. So much of our work at present involves telling the student what geographers think has happened, and consequently the student's ideas lack the freshness and vitality of ideas produced through guided personal discovery. In this way we hope that pupils will learn to think as geographers think, and not just to repeat what other geographers have found out. In much of this work, therefore, the teacher will find himself actively participating with his students in the formulation of the group's ideas in a particular field.

This approach might appear very time-consuming, but this is not so in the long run, for concepts discovered in this way are really learnt and can be applied by the student to a wide variety of similar situations, both in geography and in related subjects. Simple mathematical ideas and statistical techniques are used to demonstrate the validity of the generalisations made, and to create conceptual models which can be used in other fields of study. The use of basic mathematical concepts is thought to be fundamental to the understanding of spatial relationships, and few of these will present any real difficulty to the average student.

Throughout the book the student is encouraged to pursue his own interests by reading the references given in each chapter. These are divided into two parts: the first, under the heading 'Read', contains references that are short, specific and essential: the second, under 'Further reading' lists books which are less essential but cover a wider field, or develop the subject more deeply, to suit the interests of individual pupils. A list of suggested library books to cover the course is provided at the end.

Suggested essay titles are given on p. 133.

In the writing of this book we have been greatly indebted to the ideas given at the courses held at Madingley Hall by the Cambridge Board of Extra-mural Studies organised by R. J. Chorley and Professor P. Haggett. We owe a special debt of gratitude to our long-suffering lower sixth-forms at City of London and Haberdashers' Schools and at St Dunstan's College. They have followed our work with surprising forbearance and have been most helpful with their comments on the material placed before them. Much of our work has been influenced by the approach used in the American 'High Schools Geography Project', and we have used some of the concepts developed by Professors E. J. Taafe and L. J. King in their *Inter-Urban Unit* of the High Schools Geography Project.

J. A. Everson,
Senior Geography Master City of London School
B. P. FitzGerald,
Senior Geography Master St Dunstan's College, Catford
July 1968

Study guide

Chapter 10
MAP Quarter inch O.S.
  map of G.B.
  Sheet 14
MATERIALS Tracing paper
Graph paper

Chapter 11
MATERIALS Tracing paper
Graph paper
  (polar coordinate)

1 The peopling of England and Wales

The settlement patterns of today depend in part upon the patterns created in the past, and were therefore conditioned by very different standards of technological development and moulded by environments differing significantly from those found today in the same area.

Indeed, to understand the distribution of settlement as it appears today in England and Wales, it is necessary to investigate what has happened over the past two or three thousand years. Before this time Stone Age man wandered throughout Britain during the relatively warm interglacial periods, being forced south before the advancing ice sheets. However, the first obvious features left by man in Britain date from the late Stone Age. These are really only of passing interest to the geographer, and consist of burial mounds or barrows, tumuli, hut circles and religious stone circles. Most of these occupy hill sites in southern Britain. Perhaps this was because the uplands were more easily cleared of their light cover of woodland than the clay vales: on the other hand, later agricultural practices may well have eradicated the less conspicuous remains in these lowland areas. Thus remains in the upland areas are the most likely to have survived, indicating that such evidence for patterns of settlement must be treated with caution. Late Stone Age and Bronze Age cultures existed very approximately from 4,500 years ago to about 2,500 years ago (fig. 1).

For about 700 years before the Roman invasion Iron Age man appears to have been cultivating the thin soils of the limestone uplands of the southern parts of Britain, such as the Downs and Salisbury Plain. Ploughs were primitive and incapable of working the heavier clay soils of the vales, until the 'mould board' plough, which turned the cut sod, was introduced about twenty-five or fifty years before the Roman invasion. Today we can see these ancient Celtic field systems on Dartmoor, Salisbury Plain and elsewhere. Indeed, many fields bounded by stone walls in the far west of Britain may well be Celtic in origin. Some evidence for Celtic occupance still exists in the form of 'place name' evidence (see fig. 2). In England (excepting the south-west) most of these names have been replaced by names given by later peoples. They survive most often as names of physical features which were accepted by the Anglo-Saxons and Danes. In the south-west and Wales, where few later groups penetrated, Celtic place names are the rule. For more detail, reference should

Fig. 1 Summary of prehistoric occupance in the British Isles (after G. H. Dury, 1960, Map Interpretation, p. 158)

	B.C.					A.D.		
	2500	2000	1500	1000	500	0	500	1000
Culture period	Neolithic		Bronze Age		Early Iron Age	Roman	Dark Ages	
Types of earthwork		Long barrows	Round barrows		Hilltop camps and forts	Celtic fields		
		Megalithic tombs				Roman antiques		
Climatic phase	End of Atlantic; moist, warm		Sub-boreal; drier, warmer summers		Sub-Atlantic; moist, cool summers	Irregular amelioration to present conditions		

Fig. 2 Place name elements in England of British, Celtic and pre-Celtic origin

Element	Derivation	Meaning
Axe, Esk, Usk	isca	water
Ouse	us	water
Avon	afon	stream or river
Dee	deva	holy one
Dove	dubo	black
Taw	taw	silent one
Tre-, Trev-,		homestead, village, town
-cet, coed		wood
rhos		moor
barro, bre, brig, drum, pen		various forms of hill features

Note that many river names of unknown meaning (e.g. Frome, Kennet and Thames), and territorial names (e.g. Kent and Wight) are of this date

be made to Chapter 1 of W. G. Hoskins's book *The Making of the English Landscape.*

The Romans were almost entirely an administrating group, and had little effect on the agricultural landscape. For the first time we see a settlement pattern produced that depended upon 'communication', with the subsequent development of 'towns'. It was also to be the last for several centuries, for during the Dark Ages Britain lapsed back into a state of local self-sufficiency and the striking 'nodality' and 'connectivity' of Roman settlements and routes were all but eradicated. Evidence of Roman occupation remains in the form of traces of routeways and in certain places name elements (see fig. 3).

Fig. 3 Place name elements in England of Roman origin

Element	Derivation	Meaning
-caster, chester -cester, etc	castra	fort or castle
port	portus	harbour
port	porta	gate

Britain occupies a fringe position on the north-western edge of Europe and has therefore become a final collecting place of successive waves of people, and ideas or cultures. The later groups were perhaps guided from the east along the open loess corridor at the southern edge of the North European Plain. The Anglo-Saxons in the fifth and sixth centuries and the Danes about two centuries later were the last groups to invade Britain

Fig. 4 Place name elements in England of Anglo-Saxon (Old English: OE) origin

Element	Derivation	Meaning
a. Primary settlement (entry phase)		
-ing	ingas	{ territory of the people of ...
-ham	ham	homestead
(-ing is the earlier of these two)		
b. Later primary settlement		
-ton	tun	enclosure
borough, bury, burh, byrig		fortified place
bridge		bridge
ford		ford
c. Early dispersal of daughter settlements		
cot, cote	cote	outlying hut
-field		clearing in wood
-ley	leah	clearing
-stead	stede	place
-stoc, stoke	stoc	daughter settlement
-stow		(holy) place
-wick, -wich		{ outlying hut or shelter, dairy farm, salt pan
d. Later clearing of woodland		
-den		pasture for swine in wood
-hurst, hirst		copse or wooded height
-holt		wood
-weald, wold	wald	wood
-riding, -rod		cleared land
(also hosts of tree names in compound with other elements)		

Fig. 4—continued.

Element	Derivation	Meaning
e. Fen names		
-fen mere, -lake	wet place lake	⎰ normally applied to localities; if applied to settlements these are generally of seventeenth- and eighteenth-century origin
-delph, dic	ditch	⎰ originally applied to the feature, but name often
-eg, -ey, -ea, eig, eu, ea	island amidst marsh	transferred to a later settlement built in the area

in any numbers. Both groups came raiding before settling, and even during the major periods of influx, a process of interpenetration with the earlier folk seems to have been the rule, rather than a wholesale wiping out, or the enforced migration west, of the earlier settlers.

The Anglo-Saxons came into Britain from the south-east and east, penetrating along well-established routes, such as the Downs. This movement was a slow diffusion of peoples, ideas and language. Place name evidence (see fig. 4) suggests a stage of primary settlement followed by a further diffusion outwards from these locations as daughter settlements hived off, following advances into the wooded vales.

Scandinavian place names are most common in the north and east of England, where they are largely Danish in origin. The extreme north of England and the western coasts have large numbers of Norwegian or Norse elements, indicating the Norsemen's interest as seafarers in coastal landmarks. Figure 5 gives common examples of Scandinavian place name elements. It is interesting to note that the Danish elements are mostly confined to the north-east of Watling Street (the present A5 road) which was the approximate south-western boundary of the Danelaw. In the more southern parts of the Danish sphere of influence, there are many 'Scandinavianised' versions of what were Anglo-Saxon names before the Danish settlement. For example, shipton (sheep-farm) becomes hardened to suit the Danish tongue as Skipton and the English 'burgh' (fortified

Fig. 5 Place name elements in England of Scandinavian origin

Element	Derivation	Meaning
a. Elements usually applied to settlements		
-toft	topt	homestead or clearing
-by	byr	homestead
-garth	garor	enclosure
-booth	buth	centre for summer pasture
-thorpe	thorp	daughter settlement
thwaite	thveit	clearing
-ergh		outlying hut
b. Elements usually applied to physical features		
-berg, -brig		hill
-ey	ey	island
-force, foss	fors	waterfall
-dale		valley
-gill	geil	ravine
ings	eng	marsh, meadow
beck, slack		stream
tarn		lake

place) becomes 'by' and helps form the place names Rugby and Naseby. Further south in East Anglia, Nottinghamshire and Derbyshire, Danish settlements seem to have been set up alongside the Anglo-Saxon settlements. For example, we can find Burnham (Saxon) and its associated Danish settlement Burnham Thorpe in East Anglia. These suggest a process of infilling by the later group and absorption by the earlier. The distribution of Scandinavian place names can be seen in figure 6.

Using the one inch O.S. map 182 (Brighton and Worthing) trace off the Anglo-Saxon elements. Use different colours or symbols to represent the elements indicating the entry phase, later primary settlement, dispersal of daughter settlements and the later clearing of woodland. Does any progression appear in the stages of settlement of this area? Again, traces of the geology, drainage and relief could help in explaining the pattern you have discovered. Mawer and Stenton's *The Place Names of Sussex*, gives valuable help in explaining the place name distribution of this area.

This exercise can be completed for any local area but with the danger that the speculation may prove fruitless unless there is a place name authority available on the area.

Make use of sheets 11, 13, 14 and 17 of the quarter-inch O.S. maps of Great Britain to trace off various place name elements. Use coloured symbols to represent place name elements of different peoples. What

Fig. 6 The distribution of Scandinavian elements in place names (after J. B. Mitchell 1954, p. 70)

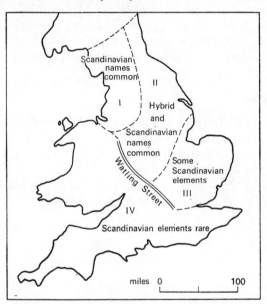

pattern of separation or intermingling appears? Use traces of geology, drainage and relief to help explain the patterns you find.

Use these techniques to help discover details concerning the settlement of your home area. For example, from which direction did the settlers come? Why did they come in this direction? Did relief play an important part? If at all possible check your local volume of H. C. Darby's *Domesday Geography* to see what parts were settled by 1086.

Figures 2 to 5 should be used with care and reference always should be made to Ekwall's *Dictionary of English Place Names* or to other authorities.

Authorities

EKWALL, E. *The Concise Oxford Dictionary of English Place Names*, 4th edition, Oxford University Press, 1960.

7

MAWER, A. and STENTON, F. M. *The Place Names of Sussex*. Cambridge University Press, 1929–30.
County Volumes of the English Place-Name Society.

Read

DURY, G. *Map Interpretation*, Pitman, 1952, chapter 11.
HOSKINS, W. G. *The Making of the English Landscape*, Hodder & Stoughton, 1955, chapter 1.
HOSKINS, W. G. *Fieldwork in Local History*, Faber, 1967.
MITCHELL, J. B. *Historical Geography*, English Universities Press (Teach Yourself Series), 1954, chapters 3, 4 and 6.
The Complete Atlas of the British Isles, *Readers Digest*, pp. 124–5.

Further reading

DARBY, H. C., ed. *An Historical Geography of England before A.D. 1800*, Cambridge University Press, 1936.
FLEURE, H. J. *A Natural History of Man in Britain*, Collins (New Naturalist series), 1951.
SCHRAM, O. K. 'Place Names' in *Norwich and its Region*, British Association for the Advancement of Science, 1961.

2 The location of villages

The siting of the original settlements in England was largely governed by a number of easily identifiable factors, although chance must be considered as a major factor as well.

As we have seen in Chapter 1, place name evidence and information derived from some of the maps you have constructed, suggests that the infiltration of the Anglo-Saxons was concentrated along the lines of the Chalk uplands of the southern parts of Britain. In this they were very similar to their predecessors in their original response to the environment. Examine closely the actual location of the -*ing* and -*ham* names on a map of an area such as Watlington in Oxfordshire (O.S. map 159, Chilterns). They are generally near the foot of the scarp face. Why should this be so?

The first settlers in a new, and virtually undeveloped environment have to exist in a self-sufficient manner. This was just as true of the early and isolated settlers of New England in the sixteenth and seventeenth centuries as it was of the first Anglo-Saxons of old England a thousand years earlier.

The first settlers, with their necessarily limited knowledge, made more or less rational judgments concerning choice of sites for their villages. Important to them was the availability of what could become arable and grazing land. In addition, a close supply of water was essential, as was the proximity of building material and fuel. Of course, knowledge of the environment was never perfect, as J. B. Mitchell says in *Historical Geography* (pp. 84–5):

> The first settlers in a place must often have made false starts and sometimes settled down permanently on a less good site even with a better site nearby, like a picnic party trying first this then that side of a bay, first one side of a hedge then the other, and in the end putting up with much that is not ideal rather than move yet once again.

In a similar way mistakes may have been made which can be seen clearly in the light of later developments. Thus we find in some areas a division of the original settlement into two, with the prefixes 'Old' and 'New' attached to the original name. An example of this is the case of the Buckenham villages in Norfolk, where 'New' Buckenham is decidedly larger than 'Old'. Have you noted similar possible cases during the course of your map work and field research?

9

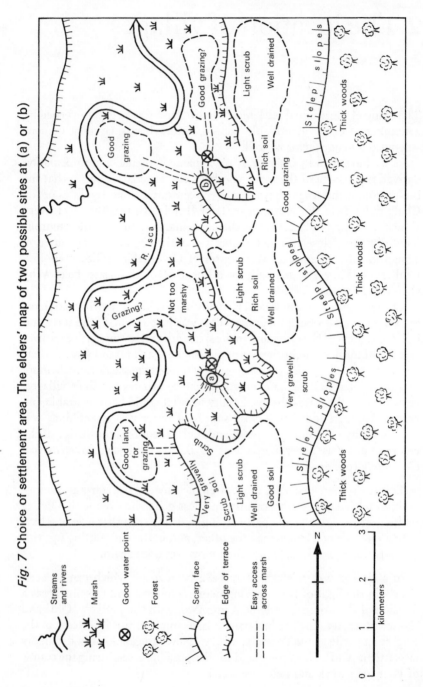

Fig. 7 Choice of settlement area. The elders' map of two possible sites at (a) or (b)

Streams
and rivers

Marsh

Good water point

Forest

Scarp face

Edge of terrace

Easy access
across marsh

N

0   1   2   3
kilometers

Despite such mistakes the distribution of villages in Britain does show a delicate response to the locational factors given above, as well as to others generally of less importance, such as defence or liability to disease. In other words, the first five factors are really the basic elements of an agricultural settler's economy. However, if the area were settled during a troubled period, defence could become the determining factor in deciding the village location. A hilltop or a meander core could become the optimum site. Nevertheless, the best defensive site would be chosen in conjunction with the other factors.

Let us assume that one group of would-be settlers is faced with a problem of choice concerning a suitable site for their village. This group could be considered for the sake of argument to be your set or class.

After some preliminary exploration of the area around the temporary settling point, a group of elders has returned from a reconnaissance with a field sketch and notes. These have been translated for our purposes and redrawn for fig. 7. As the distances to each of those areas supplying the five essential resources was not accurately portrayed and it required translation into kilometres, the distances are reproduced in fig. 8. These distances are for two possible sites.

Using the information given, attempt by discussion to select the final site which was eventually chosen. We may assume that no hostilities were expected by the settlers.

During the course of the ensuing argument, which appeared to be getting nowhere, a potential economist suggested that each resource should be given a 'weighting' depending upon immediate importance. This, he said, should range from '1' to '10', the higher the factor the more important it is to the village, in terms of regularity of use, taking into account quantities or weight required at any time.

Discuss which weighting should be given to each resource, come to some agreement, and then complete fig. 8. The site with the lowest total

Fig. 8 Distances of resources from two possible village sites

	Distance from		Weighting	Distance ×	Weighting
Resource	Site 'a'	Site 'b'	(1–10)	Site 'a'	Site 'b'
Water	0·1 km	0·5 km			
Arable	2·0 km	1·0 km			
Grazing	2·5 km	1·5 km			
Fuel	3·0 km	2·0 km			
Building material	3·0 km	2·0 km			
			Totals		

Source—Chisholm (1962)—adapted

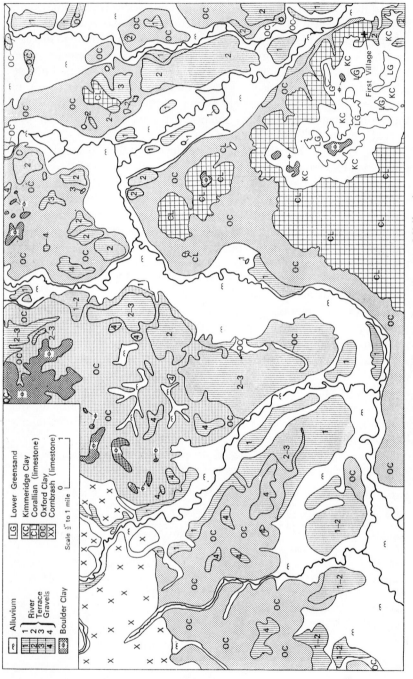

Fig. 9 Geology map of part of south-east Midlands

Legend:

Alluvium

River Terrace Gravels
1
2
3
4

Boulder Clay

LG Lower Greensand
KC Kimmeridge Clay
CL Corallian (limestone)
OC Oxford Clay
XX Cornbrash (limestone)

Scale ½ to 1 mile

0   1

First Village

is the one which is thought to be the most efficient for the village. It is important to understand that any other group (or class) may well come to a different decision. Indeed, this element of chance probably entered into every such decision made by settling peoples. Despite the operation of chance, the decision would always appear to be a rational one to those who made it.

Normally it seems that water availability is the most important factor, but it may be outweighed by the combined effect of the others. We would expect most groups of elders in this case to have chosen location 'B' – however, of course, you may not agree!

Using available $2\frac{1}{2}$ inch O.S. maps and if possible field knowledge, attempt to analyse the siting factors of a small number of local villages.

If the ideas presented in the decision-making above have any value, we should be able to predict possible village sites in an unknown area.

The geological map shown in fig. 9 is for an area in the south-east Midlands. The area is one of very nearly horizontal strata, dipping gradually to the south-east, so that lower (older) beds outcrop to the north-west. The solid geology is largely composed of alternating clays and limestones or sandstone. Several rivers meander across wide flood plains which are floored with marshy alluvium. Left high and dry on either side of these flood plains are remnants of a series of river terraces composed of gravels which were lightly forested at the time of the first settlement of the area. Small patches of boulder clay are present, and in common with the clay of the solid geology, were very damp, heavily forested, and very difficult to plough at this time. The Lower Greensand, though well drained, was forested quite thickly, and had poor and infertile podsolic soils.

In common with the social and economic background of the time the settlement was to be nucleated in form. Each settlement was more or less self-sufficient at the time of its inception, and required an area of land to support its population which produced a distance between neighbouring settlements of not less than one mile, but not more than two and a half miles. The upper limit of distance between settlements was not rigidly observed where the flood plains were wider than two and a half miles. Generally speaking, the influx of new settlers tended to move in a northerly direction, from the south-east corner of the map.

Place tracing paper over the geological map and considering the information already given about the area, attempt to reproduce a possible pattern of settlements. The network of connecting roads can also be added to the trace.

This exercise will not produce identical results from any two students. Nevertheless, so long as rational decisions are made at each stage, any one pattern created is likely to be a reasonable one, and one which could have been produced under actual conditions. In other words, the complete collection of patterns will vary between certain extremes in a random manner.

You have so far produced a pattern which depended upon your knowledge of the circumstances of the environment. This must necessarily have been moulded by judgments about the physical conditions over the whole area at any one time. Of course, the first settlers had knowledge only of a limited area around their immediate position, and therefore could not make decisions guided by what might be the state of their environment more than about five miles distant. Thus both chance and a limited state of knowledge should be brought into a consideration of a 'model' of settlement.

The following simulation approach begins with an initial settlement, the founding settlement, and then builds up a series of settlements around it as governed by a sequence of random numbers. These numbers can be

Fig. 10 Probability matrix for the generation of settlements

					000	001–003	004–006	007			
			008	009–013	014–021	022–031	032–041	042–049	050–054	055	
		056	057–064	065–074	075–088	089–108	109–128	129–142	143–152	153–160	161
	162–166	167–176	177–197	198–215	216–228	229–241	242–259	260–280	281–290	291–295	
296	297–304	305–318	319–326	327–341	342–346	347–351	352–366	367–374	375–388	389–396	397
398–400	401–410	411–430	431–443	444–448	X	449–453	454–466	467–486	487–496	497–499	
500–502	503–512	513–532	533–545	546–550		551–555	556–568	569–588	589–598	599–601	
602	603–610	611–624	625–642	643–647	648–652	653–657	658–660	661–680	681–694	695–702	703
	704–708	709–718	719–739	740–757	758–770	771–783	784–801	802–822	823–832	833–837	
		838	839–846	847–856	857–870	871–890	891–910	911–924	925–934	935–942	943–
			944	945–949	950–957	958–967	968–977	978–985	986–990	991	
				992	993–995	996–998	999				

Note that numbers between 0 and 9 should be selected only when preceded by two noughts. Likewise, numbers between 10 and 99 should only be selected if preceded by one nought. In other words *all* numbers should be selected as three digits from the random number table

found by using tables of random numbers, by extracting the last three digits of a sequence of telephone numbers from a directory, or by using the table of random numbers at the end of this chapter. There are a number of basic rules that must be followed in creating this simulation pattern. Firstly, for each time or generation, every village in the area will want to create a new village for its excess population. Secondly, any site may be settled once only. Thirdly, the distance and direction of each new village is determined by the numbers found in the probability matrix, fig. 10.

The matrix was developed with the following ideas in mind. As each village requires its own territory, no new settlement can occur within three-quarters of a mile of the generating village. This is dealt with by leaving a clear area of this size around point X. The major area of new village settlement will be between one and a half and two miles from the generating village. New settlements at greater distances will be rare, as few settlers will want to move far into the unknown and unfamiliar. Few new villages will develop under one and a half miles apart as each village needs a tributary area to provide it with food and resources. The matrix takes these ideas into account in all directions from point X by apportioning numbers in a pattern to guide new settlements to a ring about one and three-quarters of a mile from the generating village.

A few further rules are required. The first settlers would always avoid the marshy river flood plains and most would try to avoid settling on the clay lands which were difficult to drain and plough at this time. The settlers would also avoid the infertile and podsolised Lower Greensand soils but would be strongly attracted by the dry gravel terrace sites. In this way all the deposits found in the area can be weighted to demonstrate their advantages and disadvantages for settlement. Figure 11 suggests weighting for each deposit.

Fig. 11 Suggested weightings for the various geological deposits shown on *fig. 9*, to be used in conjunction with *fig. 10*

Geological deposit	Suggested weighting
Alluvium	On no occasion
Terrace Gravels	On every occasion
Boulder Clay	On 1 in 2 occasions
Lower Greensand	On 2 in 3 occasions
Kimmeridge Clay	On 1 in 3 occasions
Corallian Limestone	On 2 in 3 occasions
Oxford Clay	On 1 in 3 occasions
Cornbrash Limestone	On every occasion

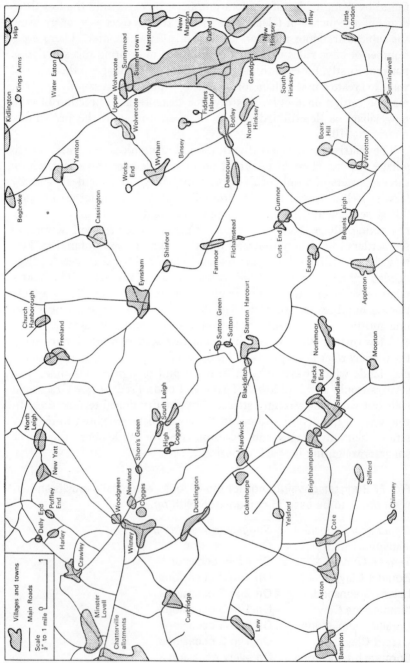

Fig. 12 Actual settlement distribution over area shown on Fig. 9

A weighting of one in three, for example, means that only once in every three occasions that this type of deposit is selected by the random numbers, can it be settled by the migrants. As is shown by the table, alluvium, because of its marshy nature and the danger of flooding, is never selected even by the most wayward of village elders.

These then are the considered decisions of the settlers. The chance element enters, in that random numbers are used to determine the village site within the constraints given.

To simulate the settlement of this area place X of the matrix over the generating village marked in the south-east corner of the map. Select a three figure random number from the table, and all future numbers should be taken consecutively in one direction from this first choice. Find where this number, e.g. 106, lies in the matrix and see where this grid square lies on the geology map underneath the matrix. As it lies over a terrace gravel deposit which can be settled every time, a first generation village can be marked in at once. If, however, the number selected was 018 no village could be marked in, as the site lies on alluvium which is never settled. (See fig. 11). If the number selected was 296, again a village could not be marked in, but in this case the selection of Kimmeridge Clay should be stored and the village finally marked in on the third occasion that this type of rock is selected. It should be noted here that any village site selected off the edge of the map should be disregarded and that if two deposits lie in one matrix square, the one covering the larger area should be regarded as the rock of the square.

To return to the first example, the new village was marked in on the terrace gravels to the north of the original village. This village and the new one are *both* used (with *differing* random numbers) as generating points for a second generation of villages and then the first and second generation and original villages are used to generate a third generation of villages. Remember that throughout this exercise no new village should lie within one mile of the nearest old settlement. This constraint may result in the discarding of a number of village site selections. It is best also to work logically through the villages from first to later generations, producing new villages every time the round of choices begins again.

In this way simulate the pattern of settlement in the map area. Compare this answer with the result of your first attempt to produce a distribution pattern. Comment on the differences seen between these two patterns.

The area concerned in this exercise can be found in the one inch O.S. sheets 145 and 158 and is entirely contained on the Geological Survey sheet 236 (Witney). Compare your results with the pattern of settlement seen on this sheet or with the simplified settlement pattern seen in fig. 12.

It is interesting to note that if the patterns produced are very similar, the generalisations we made in creating the model and matrix have been demonstrated as having some validity and the model could be used to predict future settlements of similar groups of people.

Table of random numbers

10 09 75 25 33	67 25 10 53 68	34 67 35 48 76	80 95 90 91 17
37 34 20 48 05	64 89 47 42 96	24 80 52 40 37	20 63 61 04 02
08 42 26 89 53	19 64 50 93 03	23 20 90 25 60	15 93 33 47 64
99 01 90 25 29	09 37 67 07 15	38 31 13 11 65	88 67 67 43 97
12 80 79 99 70	80 15 73 61 47	64 04 03 66 53	98 95 11 68 77
66 26 57 47 17	34 07 27 68 50	36 69 73 61 70	65 81 33 98 85
31 06 01 08 05	45 57 18 24 06	35 30 34 26 14	86 79 90 74 39
18 62 38 85 79	02 05 16 56 93	68 66 57 48 18	72 05 38 52 47
63 57 33 21 35	05 32 54 70 48	90 55 35 75 48	28 46 32 87 09
73 79 64 57 53	03 52 96 47 78	35 80 83 42 82	60 93 52 03 44
98 52 01 77 67	14 90 56 86 07	22 10 94 05 58	60 97 09 34 33
11 80 50 54 31	39 80 82 77 32	50 72 56 83 48	29 40 52 42 01
82 45 29 96 34	06 28 89 80 83	13 74 67 00 78	18 47 54 06 10
88 68 54 02 00	86 50 75 84 01	36 76 66 79 51	90 36 47 64 93
99 59 46 73 48	87 51 76 49 69	91 82 60 89 28	93 78 56 13 68
39 00 35 04 12	11 23 18 83 35	50 52 68 29 23	29 82 08 43 17
19 40 62 49 27	50 77 71 60 47	27 29 03 62 17	92 30 38 12 38
07 56 17 91 83	49 16 36 76 68	91 97 85 56 84	39 78 78 10 41
45 65 06 59 33	70 32 79 24 35	98 51 17 62 13	40 14 96 94 54
21 38 38 40 28	81 55 60 05 21	65 37 26 64 43	44 63 55 18 98
65 80 74 69 09	48 12 35 91 88	11 43 09 63 22	76 56 93 68 05
74 35 17 03 05	17 17 77 66 14	46 72 40 25 22	85 70 27 22 56
09 80 72 91 85	50 15 14 48 14	58 45 43 36 46	04 31 23 93 42
77 82 60 68 75	69 23 02 72 67	74 74 10 03 88	73 21 45 76 96
03 11 52 62 29	95 57 16 11 77	71 82 42 39 88	86 53 37 90 22
91 49 91 45 23	68 47 92 76 86	46 16 28 35 54	94 75 08 99 23
80 33 69 45 98	26 94 03 68 58	70 29 73 41 35	53 14 03 33 40
44 10 48 19 49	85 15 74 79 54	32 97 92 65 75	57 60 04 08 81
12 55 07 37 42	11 10 00 20 40	12 86 07 46 97	96 64 48 94 39
63 60 64 93 29	16 50 53 44 84	40 21 95 25 63	43 05 17 70 82

Read

CHISHOLM, M. *Rural Settlement and Land Use*, Hutchinson's University Library, 1962, chapter 6.

DURY, G. H. *Map Interpretation*, chapter 11.

HOSKINS, W. G. *The Making of the English Landscape*, chapter 2.

MITCHELL, J. B. *Historical Geography*, chapter 4.

Further reading

ORWIN, C. S. and ORWIN, C. S. *The Open Fields*, 2nd edn. Oxford University Press, 1954, early chapters.

On the creation of probability matrices

CHORLEY, R. J. and HAGGETT, P., eds. *Models in Geography*, Methuen, 1967, chapter 14.

HAGGETT, P. *Locational Analysis in Human Geography*, Arnold, 1965, pp. 97 and 305.

MORRILL, R. L. *Simulation of Central Place Patterns Over Time*, Lund Studies in Geography, Series B, No. 26, 1965.

3 Parish size and shape

In chapters 1 and 2, it has been seen how the Anglo-Saxons moved into England and Wales during the sixth and seventh centuries, and how the location of their settlements was governed by reasonably rational judgments concerned with the availability of local material resources. Once settled, the village groups had to use the materials provided by the immediately surrounding countryside to support themselves. They were of course virtually self-sufficient communities requiring shelter and protection, supplies of food, fuel and materials for clothing.

Considering these ideas, it is not difficult to realise that each community had to draw upon a tributary area for its support, and that under unchanging conditions this area had to be of a minimum size to support the people living in the village. This area also imposes a maximum limit on the population of the village by limiting the materials, food, fuel, etc. that can be supplied. This restriction can be removed by an advance in technology which could alter the intensity of land use or

Fig. 13 Packing problems of circular parishes

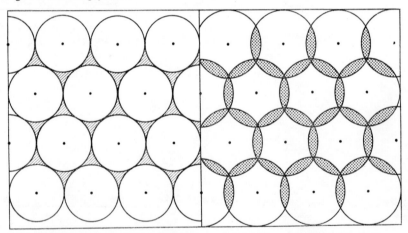

A: Circular parishes around villages
leaving areas not taken up

B. Circular parishes around villages
with over-lapping areas

the availability of a resource. In the simulation exercise in chapter 2 this control was recognised by imposing a limit on the closeness of neighbouring settlements.

In examining the area required to supply one settlement, it is reasonable to assume that it will be more or less circular in shape. That is, if it is assumed that the village is located on a featureless plain with no differences of soils, relief, climate, accessibility, etc. and with no near neighbouring villages. If now this featureless plain or 'isotropic surface' is colonised by a large number of settlements, the territory of each settlement will grow outwards until it meets the territory of the neighbouring villages. These original boundaries are shown approximately on our presentday Ordnance Survey maps as parish boundaries. The parish boundaries will not of course be circular as can easily be proved by drawing circles around the villages, see fig. 13. It can clearly be seen that circles do not pack as they either overlap or leave gaps between themselves. Consequently although circles represent the shortest, and therefore quickest, distance from the central point or village to the edges of the territory, they are not usually seen as parish shapes.

What pattern of village distribution would be expected on this featureless plain that allows the greatest density of settlement to occur? The

Fig. 14 Villages located at the vertices of equilateral triangles

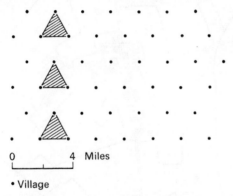

0   4   Miles

• Village

pattern that allows the most villages in the area will be the one seen in fig. 14 where the villages are found at the vertices of equilateral triangles. What parish shape would be expected in an area settled in the manner of fig. 14 to allow the shortest distance from the village to the edges of its territory (parish) and one that leaves no part of the area outside a parish?

An experiment first used by Dr M. A. Morgan of Bristol University can be made to test these ideas. Take a large sheet of *pink* blotting paper which will be assumed to be the featureless plain described earlier. Using a pencil, mark on the blotting paper the location of villages as in fig. 14, two miles apart at a scale of one inch to one mile. At the site of each settlement make a small hole into which a tightly rolled piece of blotting

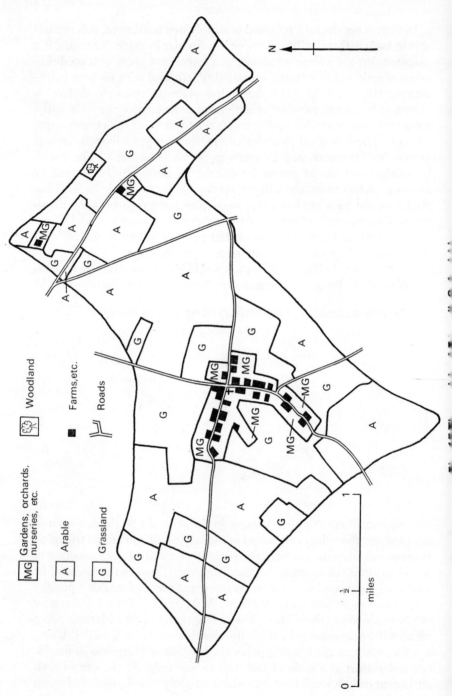

paper should be inserted. The wicks should be about one and a half inches long and all should extend downwards for the same distance. The sheet with the wicks downwards should be placed over a shallow dish which contains n-butanol alcohol. If the experiment is carried out properly the alcohol should rise up the wicks and spread out into the blotting paper. When the blotting paper between all the settlements has become saturated, the paper should be removed and allowed to dry. What shape are the boundaries between the settlements which are marked by the red dye? The shape of the boundaries marked by the dye was caused by the alcohol carrying the colour outwards from the village. As the alcohol has the property of moving at a constant speed, the boundary around a centre represents a line of nearly equal time and distance from the village. The hexagonal pattern of parishes produced on the paper is the ideal shape for parishes as they are the nearest shape to a circle that covers the entire area.

What three main factors determine the actual size of the area required to serve the central settlement? Will the intensity of land use throughout the hypothetical parish be constant from the centre to the periphery? If not, why not?

Figure 15 (at a scale of two inches to one mile) and Figure 16 (at a scale of two and a half inches to one mile) show the land use of two villages and their parishes. The land use is taken from the original One Inch Land Utilisation Survey of the 1930s. Fritwell, in Oxfordshire, can be found on sheet 94, and Brinkhill, in Lincolnshire, on sheet 40/48 of the Land Utilisation Survey maps. Place a sheet of tracing paper (preferably tracing graph paper) over the maps and on it draw concentric rings with radii of one tenth of a mile, two tenths of a mile, three tenths of a mile and so on until all the map is covered by rings. The main road junction should be taken as the centre of the parish for the purpose of this exercise. Four main categories of land use are shown on the maps – arable, grassland, woodland and intensive small holdings. Taking each ring in turn, there will be about seventeen on the Brinkhill map and slightly less on the other, estimate the percentage of each category in each ring.

The estimation is much easier if tracing graph paper is used but still can be done with ordinary tracing paper. The results should be tabulated for each ring and line graphs or histograms can be constructed to show the variations more clearly. The x-axis should be used for the distance from the village and the y-axis for the percentage of each category. Individual graphs may be used for each category of land use, or all the categories may be placed on one graph. In this case the y-axis should be graduated in percentages to 100 per cent.

Fig. 16 The parish of Brinkhill, Lincolnshire

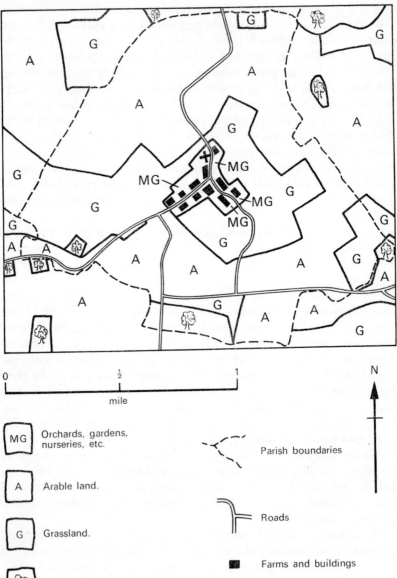

MG   Orchards, gardens, nurseries, etc.

A   Arable land.

G   Grassland.

🌳   Woodland

Parish boundaries

Roads

■   Farms and buildings

N

0   ½   1

mile

What observations can now be made about the land use patterns of these parishes?

Figure 17 shows the land use for a small area around Maltby le Marsh

Fig. 17 Land use of part of Maltby le Marsh, Lincolnshire

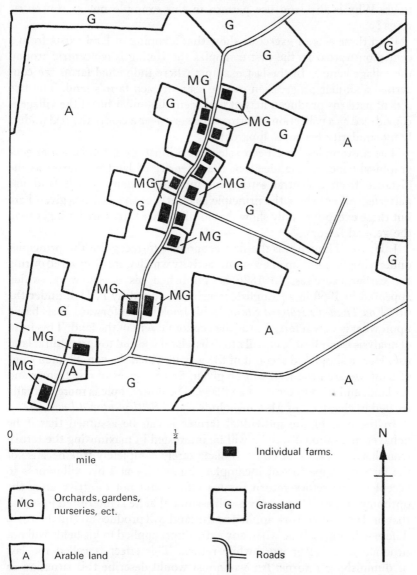

in Lincolnshire. As before the land use information has been derived from the Land Utilisation map sheet 40/48. In this case there are a number of farms sited along a road and their farmland extends into the fens from the road. Does a similar pattern to the one discovered around Fritwell and Brinkhill exist in this area? Methods similar to the concentric rings used earlier can be employed to quantify the observations. Why is the land use pattern in this example not in concentric rings ?

Both these sets of exercises show that a zoning of land exists from a centre outwards. In the first examples the zoning is concentric around the village centre. In the last example where individual farms are concerned a similar progression can be seen in each farm's land. The two sets of patterns produced may at first seem dissimilar but if the village is considered as a collection of farms at or very near a centre the real underlying similarity becomes apparent.

These examples have been selected to illustrate a fundamental geographical concept, the idea that the intensity of land use varies as the distance from a central settlement increases. Many parish land use patterns will not show the principle as clearly as the parishes given here but these exceptions only show that locally other forces are stronger than the general factors.

J. H. von Thunen was the first economist to recognise the principles underlying the location of economic activity which were discovered during the earlier exercises. In 1826 he published his classic work, which appeared in 1966 in an English translation edited by P. Hall under the title *Von Thunen's Isolated State*. In his book he put forward ideas based upon what is now referred to as the economic rent of the land. This form of analysis is applicable equally to urban land use and to agricultural land use. Here a simplified account of the way in which the von Thunen rings of land use are produced will be given, first in terms of one farmer and his land, and then in terms of a village. The entire topic is more formally treated in chapter 2 of M. Chisholm's *Rural Settlement and Land Use.*

In the case of the individual farmer it can be assumed that if he behaves in a rational way he will be interested in maximising the return from his application of effort. This is rarely completely true because of the farmer's imperfect or incomplete knowledge and his willingness to accept a satisfactory return for his efforts and not to strive after the optimum return. However, we will assume that he is interested in seeing that his last unit of work applied to the land will produce an equal return. There will come a time when any extra effort applied to his fields will not produce an equal or worthwhile return. This effect is called the law of diminishing returns. An economist would describe this situation as occurring when the cost of the last or marginal unit of labour applied to the field in question exceeds the value of the last or marginal unit of return from that field. The farmer will then stop his work and turn elsewhere, to land where he may make a reasonable return. Of course most farmers are not gifted with perfect judgment and individuals will err on either side of a middle course or 'norm', but most farmers will group closely around this average result to make these observations valid.

The farther the land to be farmed is from the farm buildings, the longer it will take the farmer to reach his fields. In order to apply the same amount of work to the land at the greatest distance as is applied to the nearest land, he must allow for the extra time taken to travel to and from these fields. Therefore each extra hour worked on this more distant land costs him more in time and energy than each extra hour on the land close to his farm buildings. Thus the law of diminishing returns will come into operation much earlier on the more distant fields which require more *total* effort to produce a similar return. This will mean that the farmer will accept a less intensive use of the land further away from his farm buildings to cut down the costs of using it.

Using ideas more closely related to the economists' view of economic rent the variation in land use can be expressed in another way. Figure 18

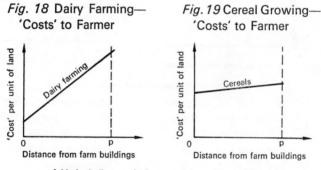

Fig. 18 Dairy Farming— 'Costs' to Farmer

Fig. 19 Cereal Growing— 'Costs' to Farmer

'p' in both diagrams indicates periphery of farm land

High rate of increase in cost per unit area with increasing distance from farm buildings

Low rate of increase in cost per unit area with increasing distance from farm buildings

indicates in a general way that the costs per unit of production incurred in dairy farming increase rapidly with distance from the farm building. Costs need not be in money terms only but can include the time lost in travelling to and from the fields, the trouble in rounding up the cattle for milking and supplying them with winter feed, etc.

On the other hand figure 19 shows a similar situation in arable farming, in this case a cereal such as wheat or barley. The gradient of this graph is less than the earlier one and the cost to the farmer does not increase so rapidly with distance from the farm buildings. Arable crops, of course, do not need the frequency of attention that dairy cattle demand. Thus a cereal crop grown at the edges of the farmer's land will not involve him in any significantly greater cost than the growing of the same cereal near to his farm buildings.

If, instead of looking at costs, we look at this problem in terms of return to the farmer, it can be seen that because of the rapidly increasing costs with increasing distance from the farm buildings, the return from dairy farming will be much greater per unit of land near to the farm buildings than at the edges of the farmer's land. In fig. 20 this idea is

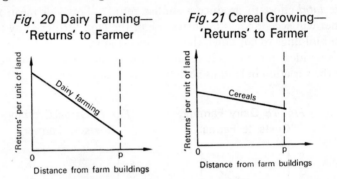

Fig. 20 Dairy Farming— 'Returns' to Farmer

Fig. 21 Cereal Growing— 'Returns' to Farmer

'p' in both diagrams indicates periphery of farm land

High rate of decrease of return per unit of land with increase in distance from farm buildings

Low rate of decrease of return per unit of land with increase in distance from farm buildings

graphically shown. It could be said that in this case the friction of distance is very great and causes a relatively sharp falling off in the farmer's return. On the other hand reference to fig. 21 shows that the

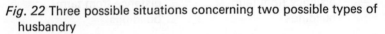

Fig. 22 Three possible situations concerning two possible types of husbandry

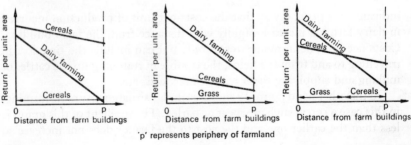

'p' represents periphery of farmland

return from the cereal will only fall off slowly with distance. The friction of distance is relatively low here.

If now these two graphs are superimposed, three possible situations become apparent as in fig. 22. In the first case with relatively high market prices for arable products the farmer, if he acts rationally and with reasonable knowledge about prices and trends, will probably opt to put his land under the plough. In the second case, with a changed market situation, the returns from grazing dairy cattle are so much greater that the farm land is likely to be dominated by grassland. In the last example the returns to be derived from pastoral and arable are so close that near to the farm building the farmer is likely to leave his fields for dairy cattle, but towards the edges it will pay him to grow cereals. This is a rather special case, which might be termed marginal, in that other factors may become locally important. Such factors could be local variations in relief, soils, micro-climate and so on.

Fig. 23 The development of three land use zones from three return curves

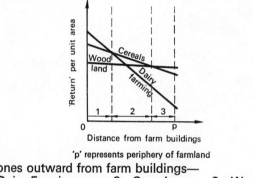

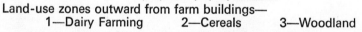

'p' represents periphery of farmland

Land-use zones outward from farm buildings—
1—Dairy Farming   2—Cereals   3—Woodland

This argument can be taken one stage further with reference to fig. 23 where an additional return curve for woodland has been added to those of fig. 22. It can be seen here that three or more zones of land use intensity can be produced. This is ideally shown in fig. 24, where under suitable market conditions three rings can be found round a village or a single farm. Thus it can be seen that villages or farms located in a relatively uniform environment can cause a variation in land use patterns.

The position of variations of climate, soils, relief (slope and aspect, etc.) and other physical factors have been mentioned earlier. It is not denied that these play an extremely important role in determining land use patterns, though perhaps they are less important than they were. Their effects may be looked upon as additions to the costs the farmer has to face and they therefore lessen his returns. These additions to cost will not be equally applicable to each type of farming. For example an area of slightly greater rainfall is likely to prove more costly to cereal growers than to dairy farmers and cause the total returns for arable farming to drop below those for dairy farming. The farmers in this case will be likely to specialise in dairy farming. Even today, when government policies play an overwhelming part in determining land use, a broad von Thunen type pattern of farming in the British Isles can be seen.

The land use survey used as the basis of figs. 15, 16 and 17 was carried out under the direction of the late Sir Dudley Stamp during the early 1930s. This was still largely a time of horsedrawn ploughs and some difficulty of transport in rural areas. Since those days the friction of distance has decreased with the development of a speedy and more flexible road

Fig. 24 The hypothetical pattern of land use developed around a village (which may be considered as a collection of farms). A dispersion of farms towards that periphery of the parish would affect the overall intensity of land use in it. What would the effect be? (See chapter 4)

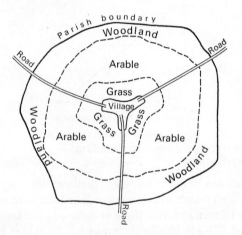

traffic, with daily milk collections and efficient transport and delivery of agricultural produce throughout almost the whole of Britain. In addition, government subsidies of various types have been given differentially to various parts of the country and differentially also in terms of the type of husbandry. Whether it has been in the form of tax and rate reliefs, guaranteed prices or direct subsidies, the result has been to blur the variations in intensity of land use developed through variations in distance from a central place.

Blurred though this phenomenon is in a developed country, it is still discernible at a local level. However, it can be considered still to be very important on a world scale, where distances of thousands of miles may be involved in moving farm produce to the large concentrations of population which provide the markets. In less developed countries the pattern is still clearly visible on the map. The less developed technology still maintains a high friction of distance. M. D. Chisholm deals with a number of examples in chapter 6 of his book *Rural Settlement and Land Use.*

As has been stated, the physical environment was a most important factor to the early settlers, to whom government activity was unknown. Within the framework suggested by von Thunen type analysis it can be said that the form of the parish which can be seen today, is but a preserved relic related to past agricultural practices, which in turn were closely related to the physical landscape and to the state of cultural and technological development attained by the early settlers.

C. S. Orwin, in *The Open Field* (second edition, p. 24), says:

Assuming the accuracy of the theory that farming began upon the plateaux and hills, there had now been a great extension of agriculture into the valleys and plains. Much more than this, it can be said that the English people of Saxon times had advanced so far in their methods of land-reclamation and farming practice that today a thousand parishes bear witness to their skill in land-utilisation. The layout of the land in townships for occupation by communities of men, which culminated in the setting of parish bounds, was effected long before the Norman Conquest, and over most of rural England it so remains. A study of the map in any region of hill and valley shows how parish boundaries were defined by farming considerations. Taking extreme examples so as to demonstrate the point more clearly, it may be shown how the need for shelter, for water, for grazing-land and land for tillage, in the proportions necessary to sustain the community, determined the size and shape of the allocation of land which came, ultimately, to form the parish.

He goes on to examine these ideas as applied to an area across the Lincolnshire Escarpment to the south of Lincoln, and an area of the Berkshire Downs.

In the areas suggested below, on the one inch Ordnance Survey sheets, trace off the parish boundaries, the villages, and major physical features (rivers, escarpments, incised valleys, etc.).

O.S. Sheet 80 – Kirkcudbright. The Machars Peninsula.

O.S. Sheet 90 – Wensleydale. The area of the 10 km square SD 97.

O.S. Sheet 113 – Lincoln and Grantham. The area to the south of

Lincoln within the arc of the River Witham and to the north of Northing 56.

O.S. Sheet 135 – Cambridge. The area to the east and north-east of Cambridge itself.

O.S. Sheet 114 – Boston and Skegness. An area within approximately 5 miles of Horncastle.

Use the ideas suggested by Orwin as a basis for a discussion of the various features of the parishes seen on your traces. Why do the parishes vary so much in size and shape ? Why are some parishes so much longer ? To assist in this answer mark on your traces of sheets 113 and 135 all place names in the parishes that include 'fen' or 'heath'. For similar reasons mark on your trace from sheet 90 all 'moor' and 'common' names. What does the distribution of these names suggest about the agricultural organisation of these areas ? The ten mile to one inch Geological Map of Great Britain should be consulted in answering this question. Measure the maximum and minimum distances from the village to the parish boundaries for each of the traces that have been made. Tabulate the average distances for each area studied. Compare your answers with data for Lincolnshire quoted by Chisholm in chapter 7 of *Rural Settlement and Land Use*. Comment on the distribution of the largest and smallest parishes in the areas you have studied. Assume that all the land of the parishes near Horncastle on sheet 114 was farmed from the beginning of the settlement. The average maximum distance from village to parish boundary in this case is a little over 1·5 miles or 2·5 km. If this distance is taken as the limit of the area encompassed by the farming practices of this time, what does this suggest about the use made of areas with fen, common, heath or moor names which often lie well outside a distance of 1·5 miles or 2·5 km ? Where these fen or heath areas have been reclaimed for active farming what changes have been made in the settlement pattern within the parish?

Prediction is very important as an aspect of a geographer's work. It is interesting to predict (or in this case to postdict) the shape of parishes by examining the distribution of nucleated villages. Areas which do not have a dominantly nucleated pattern of settlement will not react easily to the following exercise.

Select an area, on a scale of one inch to one mile, perhaps one of the areas analysed earlier. Mark in pencil on a sheet of pink blotting paper the distribution of nucleated villages from the map. Blotting paper wicks should be pushed through the pencil marks and the earlier experiment repeated. To what extent is there agreement between the simulated pattern and that actually found in reality? Comment upon and try to explain the divergences.

Read

CHISHOLM, M. *Rural Settlement and Land Use*, chapters 1, 4 and 7.
DURY, G. *Map Interpretation*, chapters 11, 12.
HAGGETT, P. *Locational Analysis in Human Geography*, pp. 94–5.
MITCHELL, J. B. *Historical Geography*, chapters 4, 6.

Further reading

ORWIN, C. S. and ORWIN, C. S. *The Open Fields*, chapter 2.
HALL, P. ed, *Von Thunen's Isolated State*, Pergamon, 1966.

4 Nucleation and dispersion

In the examination of one inch maps throughout Britain not only differences in parish size and shape but also variations in the size of individual settlements may have been noticed. Areas with dominantly nucleated and often quite large villages contrast with areas where the unit of settlement is the individual isolated farmstead.

The factors which have led to the variations between those areas which have a dominantly nucleated form of settlement, and those which have a dominantly dispersed pattern, are many and varied. It is important to realise that the pattern so produced is a result of a number of forces, working either in conjunction or in opposition, over a long period of time. Some of these forces are still at work, but the pattern in this country is largely a result of forces acting continuously, but with varying intensity, from Anglo-Saxon times to the mid-nineteenth century. Later changes in the settlement pattern were mainly associated with the growth of industrial towns and will be discussed elsewhere.

Man is naturally gregarious and it is useful to take this as the expected condition. In other words, one should expect to find a tendency to nucleation, if only on social grounds. This bias may be added to by other considerations, but we have to look for very strong economic forces if we are to explain dispersion.

The factors which emphasise nucleation include defensive considerations, where a location may be chosen on a hilltop, or within a meander core; and factors related to water. These latter are complicated, but where water is available at localised points, as is the case on certain rock formations such as limestone, the development of large nucleated settlements may be encouraged. On the other hand, too much water, the fear of flooding, or the presence of unsure foundations, may well also encourage a marked nucleation. To a certain extent we have seen this already in the case of the settlement simulation carried out in chapter 2, where we found a strong tendency to site villages upon well drained river terrace gravels above the marshy flood plain with its danger of flooding. Further discussion of these factors may be found in *The Geography of Towns* by A. E. Smailes. By far the most important group of factors affecting patterns of settlement are the socio-economic ones of past centuries.

The Anglo-Saxon settlers from the continent are thought to have brought with them a type of farming organised on an 'open field' basis. This may have developed from a primitive form of farming where new cultivators, with poor technology and little pressure on space, cultivated first one patch of land as a group, then moved on to another when crop yields started to fall because of the over-cultivation. The abandoned land was allowed to recuperate as fallow for a number of years. This type of farming, known as bush fallowing, is common today in many inter-tropical societies. Even within the last hundred years this type of farming was carried out in a modified form in parts of Scotland where land was taken in for cultivation for a year and then allowed to revert while other land was cultivated. This system was known as 'run-rig' and was once very common in infertile areas of Scotland and perhaps northern England.

On the better soils of the Midlands and much of southern Britain, these settlers farmed their parish land on the basis of three large fields, on a three-year rotation, with one year being allowed for fallow. The grass and stubble were cropped by the livestock of the village. There are records that in more fertile areas a four field system was used, whereby

Fig. 25 Probable extent of the Open Field in England and Wales (after C. S. Orwin 1954)

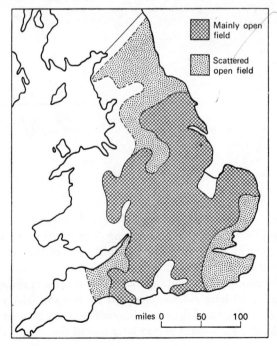

Mainly open field

Scattered open field

miles 0   50   100

each field was allowed to lie fallow for only one year in four. Similarly, a two field system characterised the rather less fertile areas, allowing each field to lie fallow one year in two. The end-member of this series would be the run-rig system referred to above, where an extended period of fallow was required. Figure 25 shows the probable distribution of open fields in England and Wales.

Reference to fig. 26 shows how the land was cultivated in strips varying in width from five to ten yards, and up to 250 yards long. These strips form the basis of our measurements in chains, (about four strips width

Fig. 26. Typical Midland Parish before Parliamentary Enclosure.

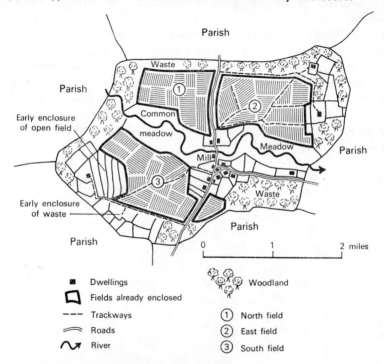

each, one rod or pole wide), furlongs (furrow-longs), and acres, which are areas equal to one chain by one furlong. The farmers or tenants were allocated a share of these strips throughout each of the two ploughed fields, allowing for variations in fertility, which were then cultivated in common. The continued ploughing over the centuries of these strips led to the formation of long ridges separated by furrows. Even today the remnants of this 'ridge and furrow' phenomenon may be seen over large areas of the Midlands. This is particularly true of those areas that always remained as grassland, and where the ridge and furrow have not been eradicated by cross-ploughing by farmers more recently.

Each farmer had a scattered holding of cultivated strips, had his cattle and sheep grazing, with those of other farmers, on the fallow field, and a number of pigs rooting about in the woodland of the waste at the edge of the parish, where he also had certain rights to collect fuel and to hunt game.

This organisation encouraged a compact form of settlement, as the centralised location of the farmer's dwelling minimised the overall distance to his scattered strips, even though many of these may have lain outside the 2·5 km radius limiting those areas of relative ease of access. Nevertheless the enclosed land around his dwelling was intensely cultivated as a vegetable plot, contrasting strongly with the very extensive use of the common waste land. Even here von Thunen principles seem to have operated.

As the population increased, so there appeared to be a tendency towards the occasional taking in (or assarting) of parts of the waste by individual farmers. The more progressive farmer wished to crop and farm as he pleased, and perhaps to breed his cattle more carefully.

Orwin, in *The Open Fields* says (p. 130):

It is obvious that cultivation spread outwards from the village, and the tendency to inclose the more remote wastes rather than to bring them into the Open Fields in the form of new furlongs arose partly, no doubt, from practical difficulties, but chiefly from the growing realisation of the advantages of farming in severalty rather than in common. Inclosures were made indifferently both for arable and for grass farming. To the progressive farmer they meant liberty to crop as he pleased and complete control of his land, free from the exercise of common rights by his neighbours. For the less progressive, farming still in the traditional way, an inclosure by his neighbour meant the withdrawal of these same rights.

By the mid-fourteenth century much of the remaining woodland or waste between each parish had been enclosed in the form of small and irregular fields. Other enclosures may well have eroded at the edges of the open fields, producing rather elongated, and often inversely S-shaped fields. For a long time small irregular plots had been enclosed in the immediate vicinity of the farm dwellings. Thus the enclosing of land had been going on for several centuries, but the effects upon the settlement pattern were only just beginning to be noticeable.

Considering von Thunen's ideas, what effect do you think the enclosing of outlying land had upon the settlement pattern within the parish? The answer is shown in fig. 27. In the case of larger parishes, perhaps in less fertile areas, the dispersion of isolated farms is very noticeable. In some cases, complete daughter villages were created. This in turn led to the subdivision of parishes. Evidence of this process is easy to discover in areas of originally large parishes. In Essex, where hamlets with 'End', 'Green' and 'Street' elements are very common within parishes the beginning of the process can be seen. 'Great' and 'Little', as in the case of Great and Little Waldingfield, clearly indicate the completion of the subdivision.

Fig. 27 Typical Midland parish after Parliamentary Enclosure. The open fields shown in Fig. 26 are outlined thickly. Note marked increase in outlying farms

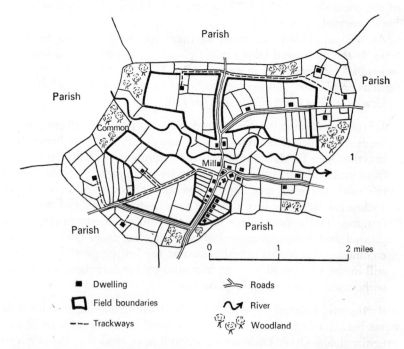

Generally this secondary dispersion was in the form of outlying farms, and is clearly seen in the case of Laxton in Nottinghamshire (figs. 28 and 29) which is still farmed under a three field system. A study of Laxton, the sole remnant of a past farming system, is the subject of C. S. Orwin's *The Open Fields*.

Between the fourteenth and sixteenth centuries, further enclosures took place as the need for pasture for the more profitable sheep farming

Fig. 28 Plan of Laxton, 1635 (after Orwin and Orwin, 1954)

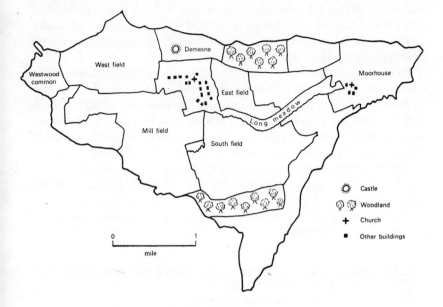

Fig. 29 Plan of Laxton, 1935 (Orwin and Orwin, 1954)

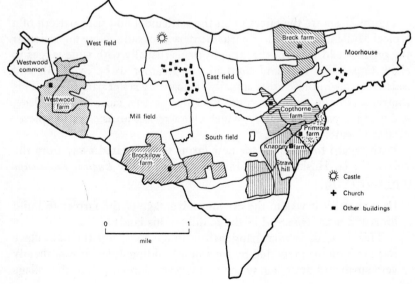

was realised. There was much legislation during Tudor times against enclosure, as this led to much dispossession of land, and together with natural increase of population, produced a large number of under-employed, landless labourers. By the sixteenth century, however, most of Britain, other than the Midlands, was enclosed.

Policies were to change during the eighteenth century. Advances were continually being made in farming techniques. Many landlords wished to breed cattle carefully, and to replace the one year of fallow in the rotation with the growing of root crops or clover. This, of course, was not compatible with the free ranging of everyone's livestock across the fallow field. Thus this 'new' farming of the eighteenth and nineteenth centuries greatly encouraged enclosure even though much money was required to hire a surveyor of the land, and to pay for the Act of Parliament necessary to legalise the wholesale enclosure of common land.

The following figures indicate the sudden increase in the rate of enclosure over this period.

Fig. 30 Numbers of Acts of Parliament authorising enclosure, 1700–1810

Period	Number of Acts
up to 1750	114
1750–1760	156
1760–1810	2,765

Figure 27 shows the effect upon the settlement and field pattern of a typical Midlands parish after parliamentary enclosure. Note in particular the regular field pattern, the straight roads (usually with wide verges to allow impassable ruts and mud in wet weather to be avoided), and isolated farms in those areas actually enclosed by act of parliament. This contrasts strongly with the more irregular pattern close to the village, and near the parish boundary, which characterises areas of earlier piece-meal enclosure.

With regard to the need for new farms to be created away from the village W. G. Hoskins writes in *The Making of the English Landscape* (pp. 157, 159):

In such cases it was to the obvious advantage of the farmer to build himself a new farmstead in the middle of his lands.

This, indeed, is what happened in due course, but the old village was far from disintegrated by such new building unless it was already very small and decaying. Often many years elapsed before the village farmers built their new houses, however inconvenient it may have been to live in the centre of the parish and to farm on the boundaries. . . .

Yet the total number of farmsteads built out in the fields between the villages is very small. One would guess not more than half a dozen in the average parish, often fewer than that. . . .

Nevertheless a new element had been introduced into the landscape in this part of England – the isolated farmstead. Nearly all the farm houses we see between the compact villages of the country between the Yorkshire and Dorset coasts date from the century 1750 to 1850. The few that are older may well be either the result of Tudor or Stuart enclosure, or examples of monastic granges. . . . But four out of five of these farmsteads in the fields are the consequence of parliamentary enclosure.

The net result of such enclosure was to create a group of landless labourers who had lost their rights to graze on common land. The creation of a surplus agricultural population and of an agriculture based increasingly upon new techniques which aimed at cash cropping and the raising of cattle for profit rather than subsistence, was to prove to be of the utmost importance during the developments of the nineteenth century. Thus the dispersion of the farms brought them nearer to the farmers' holdings, which had also been consolidated. Using the von Thunen principles, it is not difficult to see that an overall increase in intensity of farming resulted.

At the present time we can see similar effects in many underdeveloped countries which are suffering from overpopulation, where – according to M. Chisholm, *Rural Settlement and Land Use*, (p. 133):

The movement to consolidate holdings, whereby innumerable fragments of land are amalgamated into holdings comprising one block or but few, opens the way to much agricultural improvement. Commonly, this results in an increase in the level of gross and net product per hectare – intensification of farming – and a greater use of machinery, the effect of which is to curtail the labour requirements.

Reference to such problems in underdeveloped lands is made in *Industrialization and Under-Developed Countries* by Alan B. Mountjoy.

With the rise of new agricultural techniques (high farming) in the eighteenth century, much relatively infertile sandy heathland was brought under the plough. This was particularly so in parts of Norfolk and Lincolnshire (see later exercise). Earlier, in the seventeenth century, great strides were made in the reclamation of areas of fen and marshland, the prime example being the sponsoring by the Duke of Bedford of a scheme to drain the Fens, directed by skilled Dutch engineers, among them Vermuyden. This was accomplished against great local opposition as the fenlands were of considerable value to neighbouring villages, who had gone to great lengths to secure a part of the fen as parish territory.

A more detailed account of such reclamation is given in J. B. Mitchell's *Historical Geography*, particularly chapter 6. The effects upon the distribution of settlement, are very similar to those already noted above with reference to parliamentary enclosure: that is, large numbers of isolated farmsteads were created. Elsewhere, elongated street villages or droves were created along dykes. Such settlement patterns can be seen in parts of the O.S. one inch sheets 114, 124 and 135.

On sheet 113 (Lincoln and Grantham) trace off the parishes of Harmston, Coleby, Boothby Graffoe, Navenby, Nocton, Dunston, Metheringham and Blankney. On the tracing mark in the isolated farms and the nucleated villages in different colours. Also mark in 'heath' and 'fen' or 'dale' names, metalled roads, and the 50 and 250 feet contours.

To what extent does your tracing reflect the ideas discussed earlier in the chapter?

Using your tracing, construct a model for such a type of parish, that is, draw what you might consider to be the typical example of such a parish.

If such a model is to be considered valid, it should be tested elsewhere, where conditions are similar. Areas for comparison could include parts of sheets 135 (the Fenlands), 93 (the southern edge of the Vale of Pickering), 158 and 157 (the northern edge of the Berkshire Downs), and 167 (the northern edge of Salisbury Plain).

Turn now to the tracings made of parts of the one inch sheet 90 (Wensleydale), where there are nucleated villages, but with large parishes extending on to the adjoining fells. Here the land is still largely common grazing land (fells or moors), with small irregular enclosures in the dales. Again a pattern of nucleated village and outlying farms occurs.

Finally turn to sheet 80, to the area around Kirkcudbright and the Machars Peninsula. What is noticeable about the sizes of parishes here?

Trace one of the parishes, e.g. Glasserton, Minnigaff or Mochrum. Shade areas marked as rough pasture yellow, and features of water blue. Plot in *all* settlements present, as well as metalled roads. What feature helps to explain the size of these parishes? In what way does the distribution of apparently usable agricultural land suggest a reason for the scattered nature of the settlement? Even if all the land were equally fertile and usable agriculturally, why would a nucleated pattern of settlement be unlikely with the present population size?

These last exercises and questions should provide you with some ideas concerning the major factors involved in the primary dispersion of settlements. There is, obviously, a well distributed water supply which would do no more than *allow* dispersion. However the dominant factor is the nature of the terrain, its general lack of fertility, and the patchy nature of even tolerable land. Large areas of Minnigaff are too high and bleak, it seems, for anything other than perhaps sheep farming or grouse moor. Nevertheless, where conditions allow, a grouping of farms into very small nucleations is seen. These are tiny hamlets or 'clachans'. These may once have been larger, but the inhospitable conditions and low economic returns from farming have encouraged a slow drift away from the land, causing even greater isolation.

Another distinct pattern of settlement can be seen in areas such as the Prairies of the United States and Canada and the Polders of the old Zuider Zee. On the Canadian 1:55000 Saskatchewan Moose Jaw sheet and on the Nederland 1:5000 Zwolle sheet trace off the farms and the communications of a small area. Why is the settlement dispersed in these lands and why has this pattern of settlement and communication been chosen by the settlers?

Dury, quoting Demangeon, *Map Interpretation*, p. 106, summarises the patterns discovered as follows:

1. *Primary nucleation* where the village was the original settlement.
2. *Secondary dispersion* where isolated farms have grown up since the original colonisation.
3. *Old established primary dispersion* where isolated settlements occur in mountains or moorlands.
4. *Intercalated dispersion* where the piecemeal assarting has developed isolated farms at the edges of the main villages of the parish.
5. *Recent primary dispersion* where isolated farms have been put on to new lands.

The entire process has been very generally summarised by Demangeon in the following way. High land, poor soils and much available water help to create dispersed settlement while lower areas, better soils and shortage of water seem generally to be associated with nucleated settlement. Many qualifications could be made but these environmental factors seem the most important in nearly all areas.

Read

CHISHOLM, M. *Rural Settlement and Land Use*, chapter 7.
HOSKINS, W. G. *The Making of the English Landscape*, chapter 6.
MITCHELL, J. B. *Historical Geography*, chapters 4 and 6.
SMAILES, A. E. *The Geography of Towns*, Hutchinson's University Library, 1953, chapter 3.

Further reading

DARBY, H. C., ed. (1936) *Historical Geography of England before 1800.*
MOUNTJOY, A. B. *Industrialization and Under-Developed Countries*, Hutchinson, 1963, chapters 4, 8, 9 and 10.
ORWIN, C. S. and ORWIN, C. S. *The Open Fields*, chapters 3, 4 and 5.
PLUMB, J. H. *England in the Eighteenth Century*, Penguin (Pelican History of England), 1950.

5 Population and rank

The basic ideas to be discussed in the next few chapters are associated with the interrelationships and interdependencies that exist between hamlets, villages, towns and a city in a rural area of Great Britain. The area to be considered is a part of East Anglia to the west of Norwich which can be studied in fig. 31, see folder opposite. The region is about 1,600 square miles in size and there are no great variations of relief as most of the land is under 300 feet in height. Variations in geology do occur as can be seen by studying the quarter inch Geological map of East Anglia. The map also shows the A roads and the 1950 railway network.

Nucleated settlements are shown by small circles. These settlements range from Norwich, in map square J10, with a population of 120,096 to Wordwell in map square C4 with only 30 inhabitants. Despite the size and the number of settlements the area is predominantly a farming region with many farms which cannot be shown on a map of this scale. Two data sheets are given as figs. 32 and 33. Figure 32 gives alphabetically the settlements with their 1921 and 1961 population figures and the percentage change of population between these two dates. The settlements in fig. 33 are ranked in order of population size from Norwich, the primate or first settlement, to number 354 Wordwell. The map is based on the quarter inch O.S. map of East Anglia sheet 14, and all the settlements shown on the map are from this sheet. Not all the settlements marked on the O.S. map have their populations recorded in the Census returns for 1921 and 1961. They are called Localities in the Census Index of Place Names. Consequently some of the figures for say Walsham, map square C7, include smaller nearby settlements such as the hamlet of Four Ashes. This can at times be a serious problem, particularly in areas of dispersed settlement, but in this part of East Anglia the results of this effect are not too noticeable.

Divide the population range of the settlements of the area, 120,196 to 30 into four classes. Shade in the circles on the map, or on a trace of the map, according to the scale on which you have decided. Justify your decisions and discuss the problems involved in dividing up the settlements into classes of this kind.

Fig. 32 Changes in population 1921–1961 for a selected area of East
Anglia

Map Square	Settlement	Population 1921	1961	Percentage change between 1921–1961
K9	Alderford	47	38	−19·1
C5	Ampton	110	89	−19·1
A9	Ashbocking	281	255	− 9·3
H5	Ashill	542	498	−10·0
F9	Aslacton	262	210	−19·8
G9	Ashwellthorpe	311	494	+58·8
G8	Attleborough	2,453	3,027	+23·4
K9	Attlebridge	135	126	− 6·7
G8	Athelington	54	47	−12·9
B8	Bacton	585	528	− 9·8
C7	Badwell Ash	358	331	− 7·5
F8	Banham	924	942	+ 1·9
C6	Bardwell	653	592	− 9·0
J8	Barford	261	297	+14·6
D5	Barnham	381	921	+143·3
J8	Barnham Broom	347	331	− 4·6
D6	Barningham	336	534	+58·9
B3	Barrow	810	856	+ 5·7
H2	Barton Bendish	394	261	−36·0
D3	Barton Mills	464	666	+43·5
J9	Bawburgh	362	426	+17·4
K8	Bawdeswell	385	364	− 5·5
C10	Bedingfield	220	231	+ 5·0
B10	Bedfield	267	254	− 4·9
K6	Beeston	121	55	−54·5
K6	Beetley	358	491	+37·2
G8	Besthorpe	161	469	+191·3
B6	Beyton	338	447	+41·1
K7	Billingford	153	243	+58·8
K6	Bittering	337	394	+13·9
D7	Blo' Norton	259	245	− 5·4
D8	Botesdale	385	487	+26·49
H2	Boughton	215	182	−15·3
H10	Bracon Ash	272	332	+22·1
A5	Bradfield Combust	162	108	−33·3

Map Square	Settlement	Population 1921	1961	Percentage change between 1921–1961
A6	Bradfield St Clare	159	140	−11·9
A6	Bradfield St George	362	337	− 7·0
C9	Braiseworth	92	66	−28·3
F4	Brandon	2,462	3,344	+35·8
E8	Bressingham	485	620	+27·8
E6	Brettenham	75	153	+104·0
E10	Brockdish	361	416	+15·2
D9	Brome	209	230	+10·0
G9	Bunwell	738	709	− 3·9
D8	Burgate	221	172	−22·3
A1	Burrough Green	334	289	−13·5
E9	Burston	309	475	+53·4
B5	Bury St Edmunds	15,937	21,179	+32·9
A7	Buxhall	363	396	+ 9·1
K7	Bylaugh	72	86	+19·3
H6	Carbrooke	497	1,215	+144·5
F8	Carleton Rode	622	542	−12·9
K4	Castle Acre	955	872	− 8·7
G6	Caston	414	347	−11·1
K10	Catton	654	2,592	+296·3
C3	Cavenham	140	200	+42·9
A4	Chedburgh	135	218	+61·5
B2	Cheveley	599	1,624	+171·1
A4	Chevington	466	373	−20·0
C2	Chippenham	481	366	−23·9
A5	Cockfield	816	712	−12·7
H4	Cockley Cley	209	182	−13·0
A8	Combs	1,300	460	−64·6
D6	Coney Weston	215	143	−33·0
J10	Costessey	916	7,051	+669·7
B8	Cotton	403	375	− 6·9
A3	Cowlinge	406	270	−33·5
G3	Cranwich	45	45	± 0·0
H7	Cranworth	195	411	+110·3
A8	Creeting St Mary	395	493	+22·3
H1	Crimplesham	220	216	− 1·9
J10	Cringleford	261	1,124	+330·6

Map square	Settlement	Population 1921	1961	Percentage change between 1921–1961
A9	Crowfield	301	298	− 0·1
F5	Croxton	281	245	−12·8
C4	Culford	284	637	+124·3
B2	Dalham	355	237	−33·2
B10	Debenham	1,085	843	−13·1
D10	Denham	151	114	−24·5
H1	Denver	718	817	+13·8
H8	Deopham	407	476	+16·9
A4	Depden	177	176	± 0·0
E9	Dickleburgh	749	789	+ 5·3
J10	Drayton	1,000	1,346	+34·6
G3	Didlington	138	53	−61·6
E9	Diss	3,513	3,681	+ 4·5
B6	Drinkstone	397	347	−12·5
H1	Downham Market	2,342	2,835	+21·8
A1	Dullingham	645	520	−19·3
A9	Earl Stonham	602	492	−18·3
H10	East Carleton	275	238	−13·5
K7	East Dereham	5,661	7,199	+27·2
J9	Easton	241	289	+19·9
J8	East Tuddenham	390	423	+ 8·4
K3	East Walton	165	117	−29·1
K2	East Winch	327	504	+54·1
D3	Eriswell	317	262	−17·4
B7	Elmswell	954	1,177	+23·4
K8	Elsing	278	251	− 9·7
D4	Elvedon	414	370	−10·6
D5	Euston	602	214	− 1·6
D9	Eye	1,781	1,583	−11·1
A6	Felsham	336	303	− 9·8
K10	Felthorpe	298	400	+34·3
F2	Feltwell	1,317	3,192	+159·3
J2	Fincham	619	500	−19·2
C8	Finningham	340	328	− 6·5
C4	Flempton	142	151	+ 6·3
G10	Flordon	183	218	+19·1
H1	Fordham	1,461	1,709	+17·1

Map square	Settlement	Population 1921	1961	Percentage change between 1921–1961
C4	Fornham All Saints	318	400	+25·8
C5	Fornham St Martins	263	464	+74·1
G3	Foulden	269	246	− 8·5
B10	Framsden	534	350	−34·4
C2	Freckenham	296	677	+128·8
K10	Frettenham	210	288	+37·1
E7	Garboldisham	556	511	− 8·1
J7	Garveston	291	492	+69·1
K3	Gayton	696	883	+26·8
B3	Gazeley	430	370	−14·0
A6	Gedding	108	126	+16·7
B8	Gipping	63	97	+54·0
C8	Gislingham	420	329	−21·7
E9	Gissing	346	254	−26·6
H3	Gooderstone	310	337	+ 8·7
A9	Gosbeck	202	213	+ 5·4
C7	Great Ashfield	334	334	± 0·0
B5	Great Barton	666	979	+47·0
H5	Great Cressingham	286	271	− 5·2
K5	Great Dunham	329	310	− 5·8
G7	Great Ellingham	562	680	+21·0
A7	Great Finborough	413	381	− 7·7
C5	Great Livermere	213	207	− 2·8
J9	Great Melton	345	175	−49·3
B4	Great Saxham	184	189	+ 2·7
A5	Great Welnetham	359	444	+32·0
K9	Great Witchingham	460	464	+ 0·9
K7	Gressenhall	604	617	+ 2·2
H6	Griston	230	763	+231·7
H7	Hardingham	416	326	−21·6
B3	Hargrave	252	288	+14·3
E10	Harleston	50	1,809	+3,518·0
B8	Haughley	814	978	+20·1
K9	Haveringland	126	107	−15·1
A5	Hawstead	266	248	− 6·7
J10	Hellesdon	922	9,744	+956·8
C4	Hengrave	186	188	+ 1·0

Map square	Settlement	Population 1921	1961	Percentage change between 1921–1961
D7	Hepworth	390	371	− 4·9
C2	Herringswell	179	273	+52·5
B6	Hessett	342	276	−19·3
H9	Hethersett	1,119	1,613	+30·6
B3	Higham	333	205	−38·4
G1	Hilgay	1,491	1,343	− 9·9
D7	Hinderclay	236	195	−17·4
H7	Hingham	1,413	1,388	− 1·8
K8	Hockering	289	345	+19·4
F6	Hockham	443	359	−18·9
F3	Hockwold	443	359	−18·9
J5	Holme Hale	343	374	+ 9·0
J9	Honingham	306	286	− 6·5
D5	Honington	225	1,546	+587·1
D7	Hopton	420	371	−11·6
C10	Horham	292	233	−20·2
B4	Horningsheath	569	762	+33·9
K10	Horsford	668	753	+12·7
K10	Horsham St Faith	843	1,361	+61·4
D10	Hoxne	769	676	−12·2
C7	Hunston	102	106	+ 3·9
G4	Ickburgh	154	141	− 8·6
C3	Icklingham	284	374	+31·2
C5	Ingham	221	291	+31·6
D1	Isleham	1,490	1,392	− 6·6
C6	Ixworth	779	940	+20·7
C6	Ixworth Thorpe	138	103	−25·4
K5	Kempstone	33	40	+21·2
C2	Kennett	154	340	+120·8
E7	Kenninghall	891	782	−12·2
B3	Kentford	245	235	− 4·1
B10	Kenton	227	148	−53·3
E5	Kilverstone	96	84	−12·5
H8	Kimberley	162	146	− 9·9
K1	Kings Lynn	19,975	27,536	+37·8
E6	Knettishall	62	42	−32·3
C4	Lackford	157	146	− 7·0

Map square	Settlement	Population 1921	1961	Percentage change between 1921–1961
E2	Lakenheath	1,713	4,512	+163·4
C7	Langham	144	77	−46·5
A3	Lidgate	268	227	−15·3
K5	Litcham	572	624	+ 9·1
H5	Little Cressingham	1,987	253	+28·4
K5	Little Dunham	290	182	−35·2
H7	Little Ellingham	254	210	−17·3
J9	Little Melton	316	402	+24·1
B4	Little Saxham	150	92	−38·7
A5	Little Welnetham	123	111	− 9·8
K9	Little Witchingham	64	39	−39·1
K8	Lyng	294	378	+28·6
J2	Marham	566	3,021	+433·8
D7	Market Weston	215	182	−15·3
J8	Marlingford	181	309	+70·7
J8	Mattishall	687	940	+36·8
D8	Mellis	390	314	−19·5
B8	Mendlesham	934	933	± 0·0
G5	Merton	164	149	− 9·1
G3	Methwold	1,195	1,560	+30·1
B9	Mickfield	169	140	−17·3
D2	Mildenhall	3,370	7,132	+111·6
K5	Mileham	399	341	−14·5
B10	Monk Soham	233	184	−21·0
F9	Moulton	567	624	+10·1
H10	Mulbarton	469	735	+56·7
G4	Mundford	260	461	+77·3
K3	Narborough	320	423	+32·1
K3	Narford	112	97	−13·4
J5	Necton	628	763	+21·4
A8	Needham Market	1,349	1,674	+24·1
F8	New Buckenham	464	375	−19·2
B1	Newmarket	9,767	11,227	+14·94
K4	Newton	644	569	−11·7
G10	Newton Flotman	202	327	+61·3
K7	North Elmham	837	964	+15·1
E7	North Lopham	582	461	−20·8

Map square	Settlement	Population 1921	1961	Percentage change between 1921–1961
J5	North Pickenham	238	466	+95·7
K1	North Runcton	312	381	+22·1
K8	North Tuddenham	301	240	−20·3
G3	Northwold	1,105	902	−18·4
B6	Norton	718	683	− 4·9
J10	Norwich	120,661	120,096	− 0·1
A5	Nowton	211	184	−12·3
D9	Oakley	215	204	− 5·2
C9	Occold	408	282	−30·9
F8	Old Buckenham	999	854	−14·5
B8	Old Newton	649	591	− 8·9
A7	Onehouse	396	357	− 9·9
A10	Otley	537	502	− 6·5
A3	Ousden	236	213	− 9·7
H6	Ovington	212	198	− 6·7
H3	Oxborough	170	195	+14·7
B6	Packenham	829	862	+ 3·9
D9	Palgrave	693	596	−14·0
K2	Pentney	430	351	−18·4
A9	Pettaugh	171	179	+ 4·5
F10	Pulham Market	841	866	+ 3·0
F10	Pulham St Mary	984	636	−35·4
F7	Quidenham	98	515	+425·5
A7	Rattlesden	841	739	−12·1
D8	Redgrave	447	449	+ 0·4
A4	Rede	161	136	−15·5
C10	Redlingfield	147	100	−32·0
D7	Rickinghall Inferior	302	312	+ 3·3
D7	Rickinghall Superior	428	369	−13·8
E6	Riddlesworth	96	133	+38·6
K9	Ringland	236	156	−33·9
B4	Risby	347	464	+33·7
F6	Roudham	162	251	+54·9
K4	Rougham	287	204	−28·9
J1	Runcton Holme	189	330	+74·6
J8	Runhall	181	339	+87·3
B5	Rushbrooke	123	58	−52·8

Map square	Settlement	Population 1921	1961	Percentage change between 1921–1961
H5	Saham Toney	882	904	+ 2·4
F4	Santon Downham	110	269	+144·5
D6	Sapiston	174	129	−25·9
K6	Scarning	702	666	− 5·2
D9	Scole	566	927	+63·7
H6	Scoulton	224	213	− 5·0
E8	Shelfanger	308	350	+13·6
B7	Shelland	83	58	−39·1
J6	Shipdham	1,272	1,237	− 2·7
J2	Shouldham	447	465	+ 4·0
J2	Shouldham Thorpe	246	205	−16·7
G7	Shropham	280	261	− 6·8
C2	Snailwell	208	216	+ 3·3
F7	Snetterton	165	144	−12·8
K4	South Acre	97	74	−23·8
G1	Southery	1,029	1,209	+17·4
E7	South Lopham	411	360	−12·9
C10	Southolt	101	65	−25·7
H5	South Pickenham	155	169	+ 9·0
K8	Sparham	224	216	− 3·6
J4	Sporle	62	84	+30·4
K6	Stanfield	132	136	+ 3·0
J2	Stanford	110	73	−33·7
A5	Stanningfield	211	211	0·0
D6	Stanton	709	1,252	+76·6
C9	Stoke Ash	246	235	− 4·5
H2	Stoke Ferry	589	723	+22·7
A1	Stonham	129	70	−45·8
J1	Stow Bardolph	1,275	1,054	−18·0
G6	Stow Bedon	247	309	+25·1
C6	Stowlangtoft	146	266	+82·2
A8	Stowmarket	4,243	7,795	+83·7
A8	Stowupland	1,468	1,070	−27·1
H2	Stradsett	105	99	− 5·7
K10	Stratton Strawless	157	229	+45·8
D9	Stuston	162	179	+10·5
J4	Swaffham	2,913	3,202	+ 9·9

Map square	Settlement	Population 1921	1961	Percentage change between 1921–1961
H10	Swainsthorpe	250	424	+69·6
K9	Swannington	295	285	− 3·4
K8	Swanton Morley	546	1,775	+225·1
D10	Syleham	237	185	−21·9
G9	Tacolneston	308	292	− 5·2
G10	Tasburgh	356	353	− 0·1
K9	Taverham	241	1,219	+406·0
G10	Tharston	261	364	+39·5
E5	Thetford	4,706	5,399	+10·4
G5	Thompson	274	306	+11·7
C9	Thorndon	553	462	−16·8
C8	Thornham Magna	209	144	−31·6
C8	Thornham Parva	104	66	−36·6
D9	Thrandeston	264	158	−40·2
B6	Thurston	566	1,002	+77·4
C9	Thwaite	94	76	−19·2
F9	Tibenham	476	424	−10·9
C5	Timworth	172	69	−59·3
K5	Tittleshall	360	282	−21·7
E5	Tivetshall St Margaret	354	277	−24·6
E9	Tivetshall St Mary	242	206	−14·4
B6	Tostock	299	381	+27·4
J1	Tottenhill	264	232	−12·1
C5	Troston	198	1,071	+440·9
C3	Tuddenham	307	335	+ 9·1
F10	Wacton	206	172	−16·5
C7	Walsham	868	791	− 7·7
E3	Wangford	34	36	+ 5·9
J1	Watlington	590	734	+24·4
D7	Wattisfield	369	414	+12·2
H6	Watton	1,331	2,462	+84·9
F3	Weeting	312	1,069	+242·6
K6	Wendling	302	311	+ 2·9
H2	Wereham	464	478	+ 3·0
K3	West Acre	339	265	−21·8
H2	West Dereham	410	448	+ 9·3
C8	Westhorpe	164	138	−15·9

Map square	Settlement	Population 1921	1961	Percentage change between 1921–1961
B4	Westley	148	61	−58·8
A1	Westley Waterless	200	165	−17·5
C5	West Stow	167	159	− 7·2
K1	West Winch	355	1,136	+222·0
B7	Wetherden	471	431	− 8·5
B9	Wetheringsett	812	592	−28·3
A4	Whepstead	376	357	− 5·1
B6	Whinburgh	182	268	+47·2
A3	Wickhambrook	846	769	− 9·1
H8	Wickley Wood	586	590	+ 0·1
F7	Wilby	332	255	−23·2
H1	Wimbotsham	507	665	+31·2
E9	Winfarthing	397	350	−11·8
B10	Winston	200	145	−27·5
A2	Wooditton	848	1,134	+33·7
B6	Woolpit	734	963	+31·2
C4	Wordwell	38	30	−21·1
C10	Worlingworth	504	460	−58·7
J2	Wormegay	378	337	−10·8
D8	Wortham	714	545	−23·7
J9	Wramplingham	168	157	− 6·6
G9	Wreningham	361	376	+ 4·2
H2	Wretton	316	273	−13·9
H9	Wymondham	4,814	5,904	+22·6
C8	Wyverstone	217	334	+54·0
J7	Yaxham	401	364	− 9·3
D9	Yaxley	339	255	−24·8

Fig. 33 Population and rank of settlements in part of East Anglia

Rank	Settlement	Population in 1961
1	Norwich	120,196
2	Kings Lynn	27,536
3	Bury	21,179
4	Newmarket	11,227
5	Hellesdon	9,744

Rank	Settlement	Population in 1961
6	Stowmarket	7,795
7	East Dereham	7,199
8	Mildenhall	7,132
9	Costessey	7,051
10	Wymondham	5,904
11	Thetford	5,399
12	Lakenheath	4,512
13	Diss	3,681
14	Brandon	3,344
15	Swaffham	3,202
16	Feltwell	3,192
17	Attleborough	3,027
18	Marham	3,021
19	Downham Market	2,835
20	Catton	2,592
21	Watton	2,462
22	Harleston	1,809
23	Swanton Morley	1,775
24	Fordham	1,709
25	Needham Market	1,674
26	Cheveley	1,624
27	Hethersett	1,613
28	Eye	1,583
29	Methwold	1,560
30	Honington	1,546
31	Isleham	1,392
32	Hingham	1,388
33	Horsham St Faith	1,361
34	Drayton	1,346
35	Hilgay	1,343
36	Stanton	1,252
37	Shipdham	1,237
38	Taverham	1,219
39	Carbrooke	1,215
40	Southery	1,209
41	Elmswell	1,177
42	West Winch	1,136
43	Wooditton	1,134
44	Cringleford	1,124
45	Troston	1,071

Rank	Settlement	Population in 1961
46	Stowupland	1,070
47	Weeting	1,069
48	Stow Bardolph	1,054
49	Thurston	1,002
50	Great Barton	979
51	Haughley	978
52	North Elmham	964
53	Woolpit	963
54	Banham	942
55	Ixworth	940
56	Mattishall	940
57	Mendlesham	933
58	Scole	927
59	Barnham	921
60	Saham Toney	904
61	Northwold	902
62	Gayton	883
63	Castle Acre	872
64	Pulham Market	866
65	Packenham	862
66	Barrow	856
67	Old Buckenham	854
68	Debenham	843
69	Denver	812
70	Walsham	791
71	Kenninghall	782
72	Wickhambrook	769
73	Griston	763
74	Necton	763
75	Horningsheath	762
76	Horsford	753
77	Rattlesden	739
78	Mulbarton	735
79	Watlington	734
80	Stoke Ferry	723
81	Cockfield	712
82	Bunwell	709
83	Norton	683
84	Great Ellingham	680
85	Freckenham	677

3*

Rank	Settlement	Population in 1961
86	Hoxne	676
87	Barton Mills	666
88	Scarning	666
89	Wimbotsham	665
90	Culford	637
91	Pulham St Mary	636
92	Litcham	624
93	Moulton	624
94	Bressingham	620
95	Palgrave	596
96	Wetheringsett	592
97	Bardwell	592
98	Old Newton	591
99	Wickley Wood	590
100	Newton	569
101	Wortham	545
102	Carleton Rode	542
103	Barningham	534
104	Bacton	528
105	Dullingham	520
106	Quidenham	515
107	Garboldisham	511
108	East Winch	504
109	Otley	502
110	Fincham	500
111	Ashill	498
112	Ashwellthorpe	494
113	Creeting St Mary	493
114	Earl Stonham	492
115	Euston	492
116	Garveston	492
117	Beetley	491
118	Botesdale	487
119	Wereham	478
120	Deopham	476
121	Burston	475
122	Deopham	476
123	Besthorpe	469
124	North Pickenham	466
125	Shouldham	465

Rank	Settlement	Population in 1961
126	Fornham St Martins	464
127	Risby	464
128	Great Witchingham	464
129	Thorndon	462
130	North Lopham	461
131	Mundford	461
132	Worlingworth	460
133	Combs	460
134	Redgrave	449
135	West Dereham	448
136	Beyton	447
137	Great Welnetham	444
138	Wetherden	431
139	Bawburgh	426
140	Tibenham	424
141	Swainsthorpe	424
142	Narborough	423
143	East Tuddenham	423
144	Brockdish	416
145	Wattisfield	414
146	Cranworth	411
147	Little Melton	402
148	Felthorpe	400
149	Fornham All Saints	400
150	Buxhall	396
151	Bittering	394
152	North Runcton	381
153	Tostock	381
154	Great Finborough	381
155	Lyng	378
156	Wreningham	376
157	New Buckenham	375
158	Cotton	375
159	Icklingham	374
160	Holme Hale	374
161	Chevington	373
162	Hepworth	371
163	Hopton	371
164	Elvedon	370
165	Gazeley	370

Rank	Settlement	Population in 1961
166	Rickinghall Superior	369
167	Chippenham	366
168	Yaxham	364
169	Bawdeswell	364
170	Tharston	364
171	Hockham	359
172	Hockwold	359
173	Whepstead	357
174	Onehouse	357
175	Tasburgh	353
176	Pentney	351
177	Winfarthing	350
178	Framsden	350
179	Shelfanger	350
180	Caston	347
181	Drinkstone	347
182	Hockering	345
183	Mileham	341
184	Kennett	340
185	Runhall	339
186	Wormegay	337
187	Gooderstone	337
188	Bradfield St George	337
189	Tuddenham	335
190	Wyverstone	334
191	Great Ashfield	334
192	Bracon Ash	332
193	Badwell Ash	331
194	Barnham Broom	331
195	Runcton Holme	330
196	Gislingham	329
197	Finningham	328
198	Newton Flotman	327
199	Hardingham	326
200	Mellis	314
201	Rickinghall Inferior	312
202	Wendling	311
203	Great Dunham	310
204	Marlingford	309
205	Stow Bedon	309

Rank	Settlement	Population in 1961
206	Thompson	306
207	Felsham	303
208	Crowfield	298
209	Barford	297
210	Tacolneston	292
211	Ingham	291
212	Burrough Green	289
213	Easton	289
214	Frettenham	288
215	Hargrave	288
216	Honingham	286
217	Swannington	285
218	Occold	282
219	Tittleshall	282
220	Tivetshall St Margaret	277
221	Hessett	276
222	Herringswell	273
223	Wretton	273
224	Great Cressingham	271
225	Cowlinge	270
226	Santon Downham	269
227	Whinburgh	268
228	Stowlangtoft	266
229	West Acre	265
230	Eriswell	262
231	Barton Bendish	261
232	Shropham	261
233	Ashbocking	255
234	Wilby	255
235	Yaxley	255
236	Gissing	254
237	Bedfield	254
238	Little Cressingham	253
239	Elsing	251
240	Roudham	251
241	Hawstead	248
242	Foulden	246
243	Croxton	245
244	Blo' Norton	245
245	Billingford	243

Rank	Settlement	Population in 1961
246	North Tuddenham	240
247	East Carleton	238
248	Dalham	237
249	Kentford	235
250	Stoke Ash	235
251	Horham	233
252	Tottenhill	232
253	Bedingfield	231
254	Brome	230
255	Stratton Strawless	229
256	Lidgate	227
257	Chedburgh	218
258	Flordon	218
259	Crimplesham	216
260	Snailwell	216
261	Sparham	216
262	Euston	214
263	Gosbeck	213
264	Ousden	213
265	Scoulton	213
266	Stanningfield	211
267	Little Ellingham	210
268	Aslacton	210
269	Great Livermere	207
270	Tivetshall St Mary	206
271	Higham	205
272	Shouldham Thorpe	205
273	Oakley	204
274	Cavenham	200
275	Ovington	198
276	Hinderclay	195
277	Oxborough	195
278	Great Saxham	189
279	Hengrave	188
280	Syleham	185
281	Monk Soham	184
282	Nowton	184
283	Cockley Cley	182
284	Little Dunham	182
285	Market Weston	182

Rank	Settlement	Population in 1961
286	Boughton	182
287	Pettaugh	179
288	Stuston	179
289	Depden	176
290	Great Melton	175
291	Wacton	172
292	Burgate	172
293	South Pickenham	169
294	Westley Waterless	165
295	West Stow	159
296	Thrandeston	158
297	Wramplingham	157
298	Ringland	156
299	Brettenham	153
300	Flempton	151
301	Merton	149
302	Kenton	148
303	Wramplingham	147
304	Lackford	146
305	Kimberley	146
306	Winston	145
307	Snetterton	144
308	Thornham Magna	144
309	Coney Weston	143
310	Ickburgh	141
311	Mickfield	140
312	Bradfield St Clare	140
313	Westhorpe	138
314	Rede	136
315	Stanfield	136
316	Riddlesworth	133
317	Sapiston	129
318	Attlebridge	126
319	Gedding	126
320	East Walton	117
321	Denham	114
322	Little Welnetham	111
323	Bradfield Combust	108
324	Haveringland	107
325	Hunston	106

Rank	Settlement	Population in 1961
326	Ixworth Thorpe	103
327	Redlingfield	100
328	Stradsett	99
329	Gipping	97
330	Narford	97
331	Little Saxham	92
332	Ampton	89
333	Bylaugh	86
334	Kilverstone	84
335	Sporle	84
336	Langham	77
337	Thwaite	76
338	South Acre	74
339	Stanford	73
340	Stonham	70
341	Timworth	69
342	Braiseworth	66
343	Thornham Parva	66
344	Southolt	65
345	Westley	61
346	Rushbrooke	58
347	Shelland	58
348	Didlington	53
349	Cranwich	45
350	Knettishall	42
351	Kempstone	40
352	Little Witchingham	39
353	Alderford	38
354	Athelington	37
355	Wangford	36
356	Wordwell	30

Source: *Census Returns 1961*

Consider columns 1 and 2 of figs. 34 and 35. What relationship can be seen between the number of settlements and the number of urban places in a certain class of settlement?

Your answer to this question can be tested by looking at the relationship between the positions of the settlements in the hierarchy of settlements (or rank) and to the actual population size of the settlement in the area shown on the map. Draw a series of graphs showing the population

Fig. 34 Classification by population size of settlements in the United States

Classification	Number of settlements	Population in millions	Percentage of total
(1)	(2)	(3)	(4)
Total	19,790	179·3	100·0
Urban places	6,041	125·2	69·0
Above 1 million	5	17·5	9·8
500,000–1 million	16	11·1	6·2
250,000–500,000	30	10·8	6·0
100,000–250,000	81	11·7	6·5
50,000–100,000	201	13·8	7·7
25,000–50,000	432	14·9	8·3
10,000–25,000	1,134	17·6	9·8
5,000–10,000	1,394	9·7	5·5
Under 5,000	2,748	8·1	10·1
Rural places	13,749	54·1	30·1
1,000–2,500	4,151	6·5	3·6
Under 1,000	9,598	3·9	2·2
Other rural territory	0	43·7	24·3

Source: *U.S. Census of Population 1960*

Fig. 35 Urban areas of Great Britain

Settlement size	Number of settlements
(1)	(2)
Above 1 million	2
500,000–1 million	3
250,000–500,000	11
150,000–250,000	19
100,000–150,000	32
75,000–100,000	34
50,000–75,000	83
40,000–50,000	49
30,000–40,000	73
20,000–30,000	109
15,000–20,000	95
10,000–15,000	120
5,000–10,000	163
2,000–5,000	139

Source: *1961 Census*

size of the settlements as the *y*-axis (vertical) against the rank of the settlement as the *x*-axis (horizontal). Three graphs should be drawn. One on normal graph paper, a second on log normal graph paper (using the log scale for the *y*-axis) and the third on the log log paper. The log normal and log log paper that is easiest to use is three cycle one-tenth of an inch size (see Study Guide). Figure 36 shows a partly completed 'normal' graph.

Fig. 36 Rank size graph for Norwich area

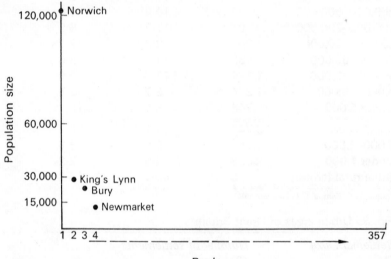

What shape does each of these graphs take? In one case distinct breaks in the curves of the graph can be seen at certain population sizes. In another case the form of the curve approximates to a straight line over several stretches of the graph. There does then seem to be some empirical relationship between the size of the settlement and its rank.

Try to discover the equations which approximately fit the straight portions of the graphs. Each of these will be a logarithmic curve of the following form

$$\log y = - mx + c$$

where *m* and *c* are constants determining (*a*) the gradient and (*b*) the value of *y* at the point of intersection of the graph with the *y*-axis. The diagram, fig. 37, explains these points further.

This type of relationship can be found elsewhere in the British Isles and the world. Use census returns for your local area or county to

Fig. 37 Graph of Log $y = -mx + c$

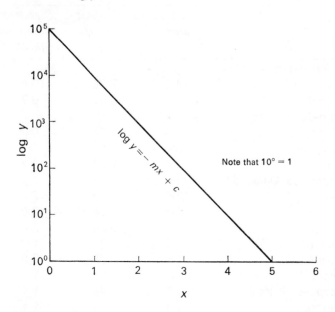

produce rank size graphs for the settlements. Compare these results with the graphs drawn for East Anglia.

One of the earliest scholars to discover the 'rank-size' rule was G. K. Zipf who wrote about this problem in his book *Human Behaviour and the Principle of Least Effort*. He arrived at what might be stated formally as the rank-size rule. This is given by the following formula:

$$P_n = P_1(n)^{-1}$$

where P_n is the population of the nth town in the series 1, 2, 3, ..., n, in which the towns are arranged in descending order of size of population, and P_1 is the population of the largest or primate town. Thus if the largest town were of a population size of 100,000 (P_1) then the second town in rank would, by this formula have a population of

$$100,000 \, (2)^{-1} \quad \text{or} \quad \frac{100,000}{2} \quad \text{which is 50,000}$$

It is worth knowing that $(2)^{-1} = \frac{1}{2}$, $(3)^{-1} = \frac{1}{3}$, $(20)^{-1} = \frac{1}{20}$ and so on.

Statistics for the major towns of most countries of the world are readily available in regional texts and in statistical handbooks and digests. Figures for the United States and England and Wales are given in figs. 38 and 39. Test the rank-size rule by comparing computed population sizes with the actual sizes of the settlements. With which definition of the settlement does the rule best fit: urbanised area, central city or

Fig. 38 Population in millions of American urban areas

Area	Urbanised area	Largest central city	Standard Metropolitan Statistical Area
New York–North-east New Jersey	14·1	7·78	10·6
Los Angeles	6·4	2·47	6·7
Chicago–North-west Indiana	5·9	3·55	6·2
Philadelphia	3·6	2·00	4·3
Detroit	3·5	1·67	3·7
San Francisco–Oakland	2·4	0·74	2·7
Boston	2·4	0·69	2·5
Washington	1·8	0·76	2·0
Pittsburgh	1·8	0·60	2·4
Cleveland	1·7	0·87	1·7
St Louis	1·6	0·75	2·0
Baltimore	1·4	0·93	1·7
Minneapolis–St Paul	1·3	0·48	1·4
Milwaukee	1·1	0·74	1·1
Houston	1·1	0·93	1·2
Buffalo	1·0	0·53	1·3

Source: *U.S. Census 1960*

metropolitan statistical area? The terms are discussed further in chapter 11. Wide divergencies will be found. Can any differences be noted in the results obtained from countries that could be described as industrial, agricultural, underdeveloped, tropical or temperate?

Consider again the Norwich area. It can easily be seen that with a primate city of approximately 120,000 people the rank-size law does not readily apply. It is far too large for the area. Attempt to find the approximate size of the primate city which would produce a rank-size curve that will best fit the curve seen on the log normal graph paper. Do not work out the expected figures for more than twenty to thirty settlements along the curve to rank 360 as a complete answer for several test size primate cities would take far too long. Superimpose, in colour, the computed points for whatever sizes of primate city you have chosen on the original log normal graph. Then superimpose the same values on the log log graph. A primate city of between 30,000 and 40,000 would appear to fit the area best. Suggest why Norwich does not conform to the rank-size rule.

As was seen earlier the log population/rank graph does not produce

Fig. 39 Population in thousands of British urban areas

Urban area		1951	1961	Percentage change
1 London	M.A	10,282	10,743	+4·5
	C.	3,347	3,195	−4·6
2 Birmingham	M.A	2,520	2,694	+6·9
	C.	1,112	1,105	−0·06
3 Manchester	M.A	2,509	2,825	+0·62
	C.	703	661	−6·0
4 Bradford/Leeds	M.A	1,909	1,927	+1·0
	C.	505	510	+0·9
5 Liverpool	M.A	1,600	1,620	+1·2
	C.	790	747	−5·5
6 Newcastle	M.A	1,128	1,158	+2·7
	C.	291	269	−7·7
7 Sheffield	M.A	744	751	+0·87
	C.	512	493	−3·7
8 Nottingham	M.A	602	645	+7·0
	C.	306	311	+1·8
9 Bristol	M.A	599	642	+7·2
	C.	442	436	−1·5
10 Cardiff/Rhondda	M.A	590	608	+2·9
	C.	243	255	+5·2
11 Coventry	M.A	515	597	+15·8
	C.	258	305	+18·1
12 Middlesbrough	M.A	483	537	+11·3
	C.	147	157	+6·8
13 Stoke	M.A	489	505	+3·4
	C.	275	265	−3·5
14 Leicester	M.A	427	466	+9·0
	C.	285	273	−4·2
15 Newport	M.A	414	426	+2·9
	C.	106	108	+1·6
16 Portsmouth	M.A	366	410	+11·9
	C.	233	215	−7·9
17 Southampton	M.A	356	401	+12·6
	C.	189	204	+7·8
18 Brighton	M.A	362	399	+10·0
	C.	156	162	+4·0
19 Hull	M.A	334	345	+3·3
	C.	299	303	+1·4

Urban area		1951	1961	Percentage change
20 Swansea/Neath	M.A	305	306	+0·5
	C.	160	166	+3·6
21 Wigan/Leigh	M.A	299	297	−0·84
	C.	84	78	−6·9
22 Preston	M.A	272	282	+3·6
	C.	121	113	−6·7
23 Bournemouth	M.A	252	272	+7·9
	C.	144	153	+6·3
24 Plymouth	M.A	253	254	+0·6
	C.	208	204	−1·8
25 Blackpool	M.A	230	251	+9·3
	C.	147	152	+3·4
a) Edinburgh	M.A	591	No data	No data
	C.	466	468	+0·3
b) Glasgow	M.A	1,878	1,905	+1·4
	C.	1,089	1,054	−0·32

M.A = Standard Metropolitan Area, C = Conurbation, Population in thousands
Source: R. E. Dickinson, *The City Region in Western Europe*

a smooth curve, but several significant breaks occur in the distribution. Norwich, as was suggested in the preceding chapter, seems to be well outside the general class of the other settlements. It could be suggested that at about a population size of 50,000 there is a natural break which separates the one city from the rest of the settlements. A very noticeable break seems to occur at about 2,000 and could mark the line separating the twenty 'towns' from the remainder of the settlements which can be called villages and hamlets. Breaks further down the graph are harder to distinguish but one appears to occur at about a population size of 570. The settlements above this break could be called villages, and the ones below, hamlets. It is important to note that the smaller settlements below about 100 are unreliably recorded by the Census returns which were used as a basis for this work. The names which have been given to the classes are of course only labels and it is quite probable that the dividing lines may be drawn at very different values in other areas. This idea can be tested by comparing the breaks in the rank-size graph of your own area with the breaks found in the Norwich area.

The four classes of settlement detected in the Norwich region are part of a larger continuum of urban settlement. The full range of terms used ranges from Roadside, the smallest, through hamlet, village, town, city, metropolis, millionaire city to megalopolis. As has been indicated earlier values for these classes can vary but in fig. 40 the generally accepted sizes are given.

Fig. 40 Classification of settlements according to population size

Name	Population limits
Roadside	1–10
Hamlet	10–150
Village	150–1,000
Town	1,000–2,500
City	2,500–500,000
Metropolis	500,000–1,000,000
Millionaire City	over 1,000,000
Megalopolis	over 6,000,000

Derived from various sources

The pattern of distribution of these various classes of settlement (city, town, village, hamlet) in this area is one of the most important factors that geographers have to study. On a trace of the map in fig. 31 shade in different colours the city, towns, villages and hamlets. Comment on the differences between this trace and the earlier trace drawn to divide up the settlements according to population size.

Considering the map that you have produced showing the distribution of settlements by type and the classification developed from the semi-logarithm graph of rank and size, discuss the answers and implications of the following questions.

1. What proportions of these settlements are of the size of cities, towns, villages, hamlets?
2. How would you describe the pattern made by the settlements as a whole?
3. How would you describe the distribution relationship between one category of settlement and another?
4. How would this distribution differ in (*a*) a mining and/or a manu-facturing region? (*b*) an underdeveloped country?

Comment on the statistics shown in figs. 41 and 42. Would you agree with the idea that there seems to be a development of town order from the dominance of one primate city over all other towns in the less developed countries, to the rank-size relationship seen today in developed countries? This idea may also be applied to the historical development of one country. There are, of course, exceptions to this progression.

Fig. 41 The number of settlements in each class of the urban hierarchy in Turkey and England and Wales

Class by population	Turkey (1955) Number of settlements	Population in 000's	England and Wales (1961) Number of settlements	Population in 000's
a 500,000	1	1,269	5	6,219
b 100–500,000	5	1,165	62	10,418
c 50–100,000	11	763	117	7,921
d 20–50,000	38	1,181	231	7,375
e 10–20,000	72	1,046	215	3,156
f 5–10,000	148	994	163	1,188
g 2–5,000	616	1,757	139	490

Fig. 42 Number of settlements in Venezuela by population classes 1936–61

Class by Population	1936 Number	Per cent	1950 Number	Per cent	1961 Number	Per cent
a 200,000 +	1	1·2	2	1·2	2	0·8
b 100,000–200,000	1	1·2	1	0·6	5	2·3
c 50,000–100,000	–	–	4	2·3	12	5·2
d 20,000–50,000	7	8·7	16	9·4	25	10·8
e 10,000–20,000	6	7·4	18	10·6	33	14·2
f 5,000–10,000	20	24·7	41	24·1	51	22·1
g 2,500–5,000	46	56·8	88	51·8	103	44·6
	81	100·0	170	100·0	231	100·0

The patterns which have emerged so far from this study of the Norwich area are fairly constant throughout the region. There are variations, the reasons for which could be discovered with further study but there is an underlying uniformity which suggests that these distributions may well be governed by certain principles of location. Of course it is highly unlikely that any observable distribution on the earth's surface will completely coincide with the predicted pattern. This does not mean to say that the principles are therefore invalid, but that they are statistical (or stochastic) ones with only a high probability of correct prediction unlike some of the exact laws found in the physical sciences. Most principles of the other social sciences are similar to the stochastic laws of human geography which we have discovered so far and will discover in the future. The variations from the predicted point out the anomalies which need further study so as to understand the forces distorting the basic expected pattern. The results of this research may result in further refinement of the principle and therefore greater accuracy in its predictive value.

Read

ALEXANDER, J. W. *Economic Geography*, Prentice-Hall, 1963, p. 534.

BERRY, B. J. L. and GARRISON, W. L. 'Urban rank-size relationships', *A.A.A.G.*, Vol. 48, March 1958, also in J. Mayer and C. Kohn, *Readings in Urban Geography*, University of Chicago Press, 1959, pp. 230–9.

BERRY, B. J. L. *Geography of Market Centers and Retail Distribution*, Prentice-Hall, 1967, pp. 76, 77.

GARNER, B. J. 'Models of Urban Geography and Settlement Location' (especially pp. 326–329) in R. J. Chorley and P. Haggett, *Socio-Economic Models in Geography*, Methuen, 1968.

HAGGETT, P. *Locational Analysis in Human Geography*, pp. 100–7.

STEWART, T. S. 'The size and spacing of cities', in MAYER and KOHN, *Readings in Urban Geography*, pp. 240–56.

Further reading

ZIPF, G. K. *Human Behaviour and the Principle of Least Effort*, Hafner, 1949.

6 The spacing of settlements

As there appears to be an order in the relationship between the size and ranking of settlements in any one area, so there may also be some order and pattern in the distances separating settlements of different size, and as may be seen later, of different functions (i.e. services provided). Refer to the maps constructed which show the settlement size and consider how the different classes or size groups are spaced in the Norwich area. Are they regularly or irregularly spaced? Is there any relationship between population size and settlement location relative to other centres of the same size, and to settlements of a different size?

The following exercises should be attempted by small groups within the class. It is not necessary for each group to do more than one or two of the tasks, so long as the results are available to all.

1. From the map, fig. 31, the straight line distances between settlements can be found.

a. Measure the distances between each town and its nearest neighbour of the same or higher class, i.e. town or city. Calculate the average distance.

b. Measure the distance between each village and its nearest neighbour of equal or higher class. Again calculate the average distance.

c. Measure the distance between each hamlet and its nearest neighbour of equal or higher class. Again calculate the average.

d. Find the average distance from each village to its nearest town.

e. Measure and again calculate the average distance from each hamlet to its nearest neighbouring village.

2. Consider the relationship that is now noticeable between average distances and the population sizes of the settlements. This relationship should now be analysed graphically. First average the population size of settlements within each class. Then plot average size of class of settlement as the *y*-axis against the average distances for that class to its nearest neighbour *a* to *c* above. This should also be done for *d* and *e* above. Plot on both normal and log-normal graph paper. In the latter case the log part of the graph should be used for the *y*-axis.

Do the results you have obtained indicate a pattern in the spacing of the settlements?

3. What factors could influence the spacing of different sized settlements in this or any other area?

4. Why consider the distances from one class of settlement to both similar and larger centres?

Figure 43 shows the computed results for the whole area. It can be seen that there appears to be some sort of order in the spacing of settlements of various sizes within this area. Similar results were found by

Fig. 43 Computed results for all area

Class	Average Distance
Town–Town	7·6 miles
Village–Village	2·1 miles
Hamlet–Hamlet	1·3 miles
Village–Town	3·8 miles
Hamlet–Village	2·4 miles

Bracey and Brush in their work on a large part of southern England. They compared this area with a part of south-western Wisconsin in the United States of America. They found that the higher order settlements (approximately equivalent to the larger and more important towns in our area) occur at a mean distance of twenty miles from each other in both America and southern England. In addition they found that lower order settlements were on average ten miles apart from similar or higher order settlements in Wisconsin and eight miles in England. These lower order settlements are the equivalent of the smaller range of towns in our area. At a lower level still they discovered that smaller centres, referred to as service villages and service hamlets, occur at intervals of four to six miles in southern England and five to nine miles apart in Wisconsin.

Many of the reasons for this regularity are concerned with the various services provided by the settlements at the present day, but much is a relic of the medieval pattern of market centres which were about four to six miles apart. This spacing was governed by the means of transport available at the time. Today, of course, this pattern is slowly responding to the influence of changed transport conditions. Further reference will be made to this idea in chapter 11.

It would be valuable if the class could discuss the factors that may distort this ideal order in the spacing of settlements.

Read

DICKINSON, R. E. *City and Region – a Geographical Interpretation*, Routledge & Kegan Paul, 1964, chapter 4.

DICKINSON, R. E. *The City Region in Western Europe*, Routledge & Kegan Paul, 1967, chapter 3.

Further reading

BRACEY, H. E. 'English central villages – their identification, distribution and functions' in *I.G.U. Symposium in Urban Geography*, ed. K. Norborg, Lund, 1962.

BRUSH, J. E. and BRACEY, H. E. 'Rural service centres in south-western Wisconsin and southern England', *Geographical Review*, vol. 45, 1955.

BRUSH, J. E. 'The Hierarchy of Central Places in Southwestern Wisconsin,' *Geographical Review*, vol. 43, 1953. Also in R. H. T. Smith, E. J. Taaffe and L. J. King (editors) *Readings in Economic Activity—the Location of Economic Activity*, Rand McNally, 1968, pp. 200–215.

7 Settlements and their services

The area under discussion is mainly a commercial farming one, and all the farms in it have a demand for goods and services, such as food, clothes, laundry, etc. These farms and the people who live in them are not self-sufficient and therefore some other place must supply their needs. Settlements supplying such goods and services may be referred to as Central Places.

The entrepreneurs who supply goods and services try to rationalise their location, that is, they attempt to find a central position at some nodal point from which they may most efficiently supply a sufficient number of people so as to produce a satisfactory profit to themselves. More will be said about this when the morphology and dynamics of the town are dealt with elsewhere, but remember that an element of competition for the most nodal points will force up the cost of land, and this also has to be taken into account. In addition to this element of competition it is reasonable to remember that shopping for goods or services is normally carried out as a shopping list, that is, the customer shops for a number of articles at the same time. Thus several shops, each supplying similar or different sets of goods and services, would be located together at an accessible point.

Fig. 44 Estimated frequency of visits to particular types of shops

Number of visits per week	
Grocers	7·6
Greengrocers	3·5
Butchers	3·3
Bakers	2·8
Number of weeks per visit	
Furniture	31·5
Radio/Electrical	9·3
Footwear	7·0
Men's wear	4·3
Hardwear	1·9
Chemist	1·0
Women's wear	0·9

Source: W. G. McClelland, 'The Supermarket and Society', *The Sociological Review*, vol. 10, 1962

If travel costs could be ignored, it would be reasonable to suggest that Thetford, being centrally placed on the map, could supply the entire area with the required goods and services. But consider the following three points:

1. The farther away a consumer is from Thetford, the greater the cost in terms of time, energy and money he will have to expend in order to satisfy his needs.

2 It is unlikely, for example, that a farmer will travel as far for a loaf of bread as for the purchase of a tractor. As groceries are frequently and regularly needed he will require a shop that sells these close at hand (see fig. 44). This minimises the cost (in terms of time as well as money) of travelling in proportion to the total cost of the articles bought. He will be willing to travel much greater distances to buy a piece of equipment such as a tractor. Here his travelling time, energy and expenditure are only a small proportion of a much more expensive item, which may well last him fifteen years or more. Thus one can distinguish between at least two broad groups of goods. American geographers particularly, refer to convenience and shopping goods in shopping centres. James Simmons,

Fig. 45 Possible functions in settlements
This table shows some of the possible functions in central places. Copy out the table and write Hamlet, Village, Town, City in the space provided using your own experience as a guide.

Function	Decision
Art shop	
Advertising agency	
Barrister	
Bingo	
Butcher	
Book store	
Boots (Chemist)	
Café	
Camera shop	
Cinema	
Circus	
Clothes	
Confectioner	
Driving school	
Dry cleaner	
Electricity Board showroom	
Electrical/TV/radio	
Estate agents	

Function	Decision
Fashion clothes	
Florist	
Fresh fish	
Fried fish	
Furniture (home)	
Furniture (office)	
Garage	
Gas Board Showroom	
General store	
Greengrocer	
Grocer	
Hairdresser (gents)	
Hairdresser (ladies)	
Jewellery	
Leather	
Marks and Spencer	
Newsagent/sweets/tobacconist	
Optical	
Petrol	
Pet shop	
Photographic studio	
Printer	
Public House	
Post Office	
Restaurant	
Sainsbury	
Shoe shop	
School (primary)	
School (secondary)	
Specialist cinema	
Specialist furniture	
Sports shop	
Stationers	
Supermarket	
Theatre	
Toy shop	
Undertakers	
University	
Wine store	
Woolworths	

in *The Changing Pattern of Retail Location* (1964), defines them as follows (p. 35): 'Shopping goods are those goods which invite comparison by the buyer so that the stores tend to group together in high-order centres, and to stress product differentiation. Convenience goods are more standardised, more frequently purchased, and seek locational advantage' (i.e. location more convenient to the consumer). Again, this aspect is discussed at greater length in Book 2.

3. There is an existing transport network of roads and railways which will influence the choice of centre to which the farmer will travel.

It is therefore not surprising that a number of Central Places of varying importance have developed over a long period of time to serve the surrounding region.

Figure 45 lists most of the goods and services that can be provided in settlements of varying size and importance. From your own experience list those functions (i.e. suppliers of goods and services) that you would

Fig. 46 Typical functions in a hamlet, a village, a town and a city.

Hamlet	Village	Town	City
General stores	General stores	General stores	General stores
Newsagent/sweets/ tobacconist	Newsagent/sweets/ tobacconist	Newsagent/sweets/ tobacconist	Newsagent/sweets/ tobacconist
Public House	Public House	Public House	Public House
Post Office	Post Office	Post Office	Post Office
	Butcher	Butcher	Butcher
	Garage	Garage	Garage
	Hardware/paint/ do-it-yourself	Hardware/paint/ do-it-yourself	Hardware/paint/ do-it-yourself
	Grocer	Grocer	Grocer
		Bank	Bank
		Bingo	Bingo
		Book shop	Book shop
		Boots (Chemist)	Boots (Chemist)
		Café	Café
		Camera	Camera
		Chemist	Chemist
		Cinema	Cinema
		Clothes	Clothes
		Confectioner	Confectioner
		Driving school	Driving school
		Dry cleaner	Dry cleaner
		Electricity Board Showroom	Electricity Board Showroom
		Electrical/TV/radio	Electrical/TV/radio

Hamlet	Village	Town	City
		Estate agent	Estate agent
		Florist	Florist
		Fresh fish	Fresh fish
		Fried fish	Fried fish
		Furniture (home)	Furniture (home)
		Furniture (office)	Furniture (office)
		Gas Board	Gas Board
		Showroom	Showroom
		Greengrocer	Greengrocer
		Hairdresser (gents)	Hairdresser (gents)
		Hairdresser (ladies)	Hairdresser (ladies)
		Jewellery	Jewellery
		Leather	Leather
		Local government	Optical
		offices	Photographic
		Optical	studio
		Photographic	Restaurant
		studio	Sainsbury
		Restaurant	Smiths W. H.
		Sainsbury	Sports shop
		Smiths W. H.	Stationers
		Sports shop	Supermarket
		Stationers	Toy shop
		Supermarket	Undertaker
		Toy shop	Wine store
		Undertaker	Art goods
		Wine store	Advertising agencies
			Circus
			Fashion clothes
			Galleries (art,
			fashion etc.)
			Large named stores
			Law office
			Marks and Spencer
			Printers
			Specialist furniture
			Regional government
			office
			Regional
			organisations
			Theatre
			University
			Woolworths

Fig. 47 Number and type of function for settlements in the south-west part of the

Settlements	Antique shop	Bakers	Bicycle shops	Books and stationery	Butchers	Cafés	Car sales	Chemists	Clothes (general)	Clothes (ladies)	Clothes (men)	Sweets/tobacco	Electrical	Electrical showroom	Fancy goods	Fried fish	Fresh fish	Furniture stores	Garden supplies	Gas showroom	General stores	Greengrocer	Grocer	Hardware	Jeweller	Leather goods stores	Newsagents	Off Licences	Pet shops	Photographic supplies	Public Houses	Record shops	Restaurants	Shoe shops	Sports shops
Bury St Edmunds	7	3	4	4	4	10	5	6	8	15	12	16	17	1	4	3	1	17	2	1	11	4	8	5	6	2	15	4	1	1	16	1	6	14	4
Newmarket	1	4	1	–	8	8	2	2	3	7	5	10	6	1	1	2	1	2	1	1	1	4	12	3	2	3	5	3	2	1	12	1	1	3	–
Mildenhall	1	2	1	1	3	2	2	1	1	3	3	3	4	1	–	1	1	1	2	–	–	2	3	1	2	–	1	1	–	–	5	–	–	2	–
Thetford	1	4	1	1	4	2	–	2	–	2	4	3	9	1	2	1	1	1	1	1	1	3	6	1	–	–	2	2	–	1	9	–	1	2	1
Lakenheath	1	1	1	–	2	1	–	1	–	1	–	–	1	–	1	1	–	–	–	1	1	3	1	–	–	–	1	–	–	–	5	–	–	–	–
Brandon	–	2	1	–	1	2	–	1	–	2	2	3	3	–	1	1	–	–	–	–	2	1	5	1	1	–	2	1	–	–	7	–	–	–	–
Feltwell	–	1	1	–	1	2	–	1	1	1	–	–	–	–	1	–	–	–	–	–	2	1	2	–	–	–	1	–	–	–	2	–	–	–	–
Fordham	1	1	–	1	–	1	–	–	1	–	–	–	1	–	–	–	–	–	–	–	1	–	3	–	–	–	1	–	–	–	5	–	–	–	–
Cheveley	–	–	–	–	–	–	–	–	–	–	–	1	–	–	–	–	–	–	–	–	–	–	2	–	–	–	–	–	–	–	2	–	–	–	–
Methwold	–	–	–	–	–	2	–	–	–	–	–	1	–	–	–	–	–	–	–	–	–	3	–	2	2	–	1	–	–	–	1	–	–	–	–
Isleham	–	1	–	–	1	–	–	–	–	1	1	–	–	–	–	–	–	–	–	–	1	–	2	–	–	–	–	–	–	–	3	–	–	–	1
Hilgay	–	1	–	–	–	–	–	–	–	–	–	–	1	–	–	–	–	–	–	–	1	1	3	1	–	–	–	–	–	–	2	–	–	–	–
Southery	–	–	–	1	–	–	–	–	–	–	–	–	–	–	–	–	–	–	–	–	3	–	2	1	–	–	–	–	–	–	2	–	–	–	–
Wooditton	–	–	–	–	–	–	–	–	–	–	–	–	–	–	–	–	–	–	–	–	1	–	–	–	–	–	–	–	–	–	1	–	–	–	–
Troston	–	–	–	–	–	–	–	–	–	–	–	–	–	–	–	–	–	–	–	–	1	–	–	–	–	–	–	–	–	–	1	–	–	–	–
Weeting Barnham	–	–	–	–	–	–	–	–	–	–	–	–	–	–	–	–	–	–	–	–	1	–	–	–	–	–	–	–	–	–	–	–	–	–	–
Great Barton	–	–	–	–	–	–	–	–	–	–	–	–	–	–	–	–	–	–	–	–	1	–	–	–	–	–	–	–	–	–	1	–	–	–	–
Northwold	–	–	–	1	–	–	–	–	–	–	–	–	–	–	–	–	–	–	–	–	2	–	–	–	–	–	–	–	–	–	1	–	–	–	–
Barrow	–	–	–	2	–	–	–	–	–	–	–	–	–	–	–	–	–	–	–	–	2	1	–	–	–	–	–	–	–	–	2	–	–	–	–
Wickham-brook	–	–	–	–	–	–	–	–	–	–	–	–	–	–	–	–	–	–	–	–	–	–	–	–	–	–	–	–	–	–	–	–	–	–	–
Horningsheath	–	–	–	–	–	1	–	–	–	–	–	–	–	–	–	–	–	–	–	–	1	–	–	–	–	–	–	–	–	–	2	–	–	–	–
Cockfield	–	–	–	–	–	–	–	–	–	–	–	–	–	–	–	–	–	–	–	–	1	–	–	–	–	–	–	–	–	–	1	–	–	–	–
Freckenham	–	–	–	–	–	–	–	–	–	–	–	–	–	–	–	–	–	–	–	–	1	–	–	–	–	–	–	–	–	–	2	–	–	–	–
Barton Mills	–	–	–	–	–	–	–	–	–	–	–	–	–	–	–	–	–	–	–	–	1	–	–	–	–	–	–	–	–	–	2	–	–	–	–
Culford	–	–	–	–	–	–	–	–	–	–	–	–	–	–	–	–	–	–	–	–	1	–	–	–	–	–	–	–	–	–	1	–	–	–	–
Moulton	–	–	–	–	–	–	–	–	–	–	–	–	–	–	–	–	–	–	–	–	1	–	–	–	–	–	–	–	–	–	1	–	–	–	–
Dullingham	–	–	–	–	–	–	–	–	–	–	–	1	–	–	–	–	–	–	–	–	1	–	–	–	–	–	–	–	–	–	3	–	–	–	–
Fornham St Martins	–	–	–	–	–	–	–	–	–	–	–	–	–	–	–	–	–	–	–	–	1	–	–	–	–	–	–	–	–	–	3	–	–	–	–
Risby	–	–	–	–	–	–	–	–	–	–	–	–	–	–	–	–	–	–	–	–	1	–	–	–	–	–	–	–	–	–	1	–	–	–	–
Mundford	–	–	–	1	–	–	–	–	–	–	–	–	–	–	–	–	–	–	–	–	1	–	1	–	–	–	–	–	–	–	2	–	–	–	–
Great Welnetham	–	–	–	–	–	–	–	–	–	–	–	–	–	–	–	–	–	–	–	–	–	–	–	–	–	–	–	–	–	–	–	–	–	–	–
Fornham All Saints	–	–	–	–	–	–	–	–	–	–	–	1	–	–	–	–	–	–	–	–	–	–	–	–	–	–	–	–	–	–	1	–	–	–	–
Icklingham	–	–	–	–	–	–	–	–	–	–	–	–	–	–	–	–	–	–	–	–	1	–	1	–	–	–	–	–	–	–	2	–	–	–	–
Chevington	–	–	–	–	–	–	–	–	–	–	–	–	–	–	–	–	–	–	–	–	2	–	–	–	–	–	–	–	–	–	1	–	–	–	–
Elvedon	–	–	–	–	–	–	–	–	–	–	–	–	–	–	–	–	–	–	–	–	–	–	1	–	–	–	–	–	–	–	1	–	–	–	–
Gazeley	–	–	–	–	–	–	–	–	–	–	–	–	–	–	–	–	–	–	–	–	2	–	–	–	–	–	–	–	–	–	1	–	–	–	–
Chippenham	–	1	–	–	–	–	–	–	–	–	–	–	–	–	–	–	–	–	–	–	–	–	1	–	–	–	–	–	–	–	1	–	–	–	–
Hockwold	–	–	–	–	–	–	–	–	–	–	–	–	–	–	–	–	–	–	–	–	2	–	1	1	–	–	–	–	–	–	2	–	–	–	–
Whepstead	–	–	–	–	–	–	–	–	–	–	–	–	–	–	–	–	–	–	–	–	1	–	–	–	–	–	–	–	–	–	1	–	–	–	–
Kennett	–	–	–	–	–	–	–	–	–	–	–	–	–	–	–	–	–	–	–	–	1	–	–	–	–	–	–	–	–	–	1	–	–	–	–
Tuddenham	–	–	–	1	–	–	–	–	–	–	–	–	–	–	–	–	–	–	–	–	1	–	1	–	–	–	–	–	–	–	2	–	–	–	–

82

Norwich area (Research by P. F. Davis, 1967)

Do-it-yourself etc.	Woollens	Supermarket	Boots (Chemist)	Co-op department stores	Co-op grocers	Marks and Spencer	Woolworths	Petrol sales	Dry cleaners	Gents hairdressing	Ladies hairdressing	Launderettes	Photo studios	Shoe repairs	Banks	Betting shops	Cinemas	Garages	Hospitals	Hotels	Newspaper office	**Post Offices**	Primary schools	Secondary schools	Estate agents	Insurance offices	Opticians	Solicitors	Class according to the rank-size graphs	Class according to functions possessed	Population 1961	Rank in Norwich area
7	3	2	1	1	4	1	1	5	9	9	7	3	1	3	5	3	2	6	2	8	1	3	10	5	6	4	3	5	Town		21,179	3
2	4	2	1	1	1	–	1	3	4	4	6	1	1	2	5	8	1	4	1	5	1	1	4	2	2	3	1	4	Town		11,227	4
–	1	2	–	–	1	–	–	1	2	2	4	1	–	1	2	1	1	1	–	2	–	1	3	1	2	1	–	2	Town		7,132	8
1	4	1	–	1	–	–	1	4	4	3	4	–	–	2	2	2	1	3	2	5	1	1	3	3	1	2	–	2	Town		5,399	11
–	–	–	–	1	–	–	2	–	1	–	–	–	–	1	–	–	1	–	–	–	–	(1)	2	–	–	–	–	–	Town		4,512	12
2	–	–	–	1	–	–	–	2	–	2	3	–	–	–	–	1	1	2	–	2	–	1	2	1	–	–	–	1	Town		3,341	14
–	–	–	–	–	–	–	–	1	1	–	–	–	–	–	1	–	1	–	–	–	–	1	1	–	–	–	–	–	Town		3,192	16
1	–	–	–	–	–	–	–	2	–	–	1	–	–	–	1	–	1	–	–	–	–	(1)	1	–	–	–	–	–	Village		1,709	24
–	–	–	–	1	–	–	–	–	–	–	–	–	–	–	–	–	–	–	–	–	–	(1)	1	–	–	–	–	–	Village		1,624	26
2	–	–	–	–	–	1	–	–	–	–	–	1	1	–	–	1	–	1	–	–	–	(1)	1	1	–	–	–	–	Village		1,560	29
–	–	–	–	1	–	1	–	–	1	–	–	–	–	–	–	–	–	–	–	–	–	(1)	1	–	–	–	–	–	Village		1,392	31
–	–	–	–	–	–	–	1	–	–	–	–	–	–	–	–	1	–	–	–	–	–	(1)	1	–	–	–	–	–	Village		1,343	35
–	–	–	–	–	–	2	–	–	–	–	–	–	–	–	1	–	–	–	–	–	–	(1)	1	–	–	–	–	–	Village		1,209	40
–	–	–	–	–	–	–	–	–	–	–	–	–	–	–	–	–	–	–	–	–	–	(1)	–	–	–	–	–	–	Village		1,134	43
–	–	–	–	–	–	1	–	–	–	–	–	–	–	–	–	–	–	–	–	–	–	(1)	–	–	–	–	–	–	Village		1,071	47
–	–	–	–	–	–	–	–	–	–	–	–	–	–	–	–	–	–	–	–	–	–	(1)	1	–	–	–	–	–	Village		1,069	49
–	–	–	–	–	–	–	–	–	–	–	–	–	–	–	–	–	–	–	–	–	–	(1)	1	–	–	–	–	–	Village		979	52
1	–	–	–	–	–	–	–	–	–	–	–	–	–	–	–	–	–	–	–	–	–	(1)	1	–	–	–	–	–	Village		902	63
–	–	–	–	–	–	–	1	–	–	–	–	–	–	–	–	–	–	–	–	1	–	(1)	–	–	–	–	–	–	Village		856	69
–	–	–	–	–	–	–	–	–	–	–	–	–	–	–	–	–	–	–	–	–	–	–	–	–	–	–	–	–	Village		769	76
–	–	–	–	–	1	–	–	–	–	–	–	–	–	–	–	–	–	–	–	–	–	(1)	1	–	–	–	–	–	Village		762	79
–	–	–	–	–	1	–	–	–	–	–	–	–	–	–	–	–	–	–	–	–	–	(1)	1	–	–	–	–	–	Village		712	85
–	–	–	–	–	1	–	–	–	–	–	–	–	–	–	–	–	–	–	–	–	–	(1)	1	–	–	–	–	–	Village		677	89
–	–	–	–	–	–	–	–	–	–	–	–	–	–	–	–	–	–	–	–	–	–	(1)	–	–	–	–	–	–	Village		666	91
–	–	–	–	–	1	–	–	–	–	–	–	–	–	–	–	–	–	–	–	–	–	(1)	–	–	–	–	–	–	Village		637	94
–	–	–	–	–	1	–	–	–	–	–	–	–	–	–	–	–	–	–	–	–	–	(1)	–	–	–	–	–	–	Village		624	97
–	–	–	–	–	–	–	–	–	–	–	–	–	–	–	–	–	–	1	–	–	–	(1)	1	–	–	–	–	–	Hamlet		520	109
–	–	–	–	–	–	–	–	–	–	–	–	–	–	–	–	–	–	–	–	–	–	(1)	–	–	–	–	–	–	Hamlet		464	128
–	–	–	–	–	–	–	–	–	–	–	–	–	–	–	–	–	–	–	–	–	–	(1)	1	–	–	–	–	–	Hamlet		464	129
–	–	–	–	–	1	–	–	–	–	–	–	–	–	–	–	–	–	–	–	–	–	(1)	1	–	–	–	–	–	Hamlet		461	132
–	–	–	–	–	–	–	–	–	–	–	–	–	–	–	–	–	–	–	–	–	–	–	1	–	–	–	–	–	Hamlet		444	139
–	–	–	–	–	–	–	–	–	–	–	–	–	–	–	–	–	–	–	–	–	–	(1)	–	–	–	–	–	–	Hamlet		400	153
–	–	–	–	–	1	–	–	–	–	–	–	–	–	–	–	–	–	–	–	–	–	(1)	1	–	–	–	–	–	Hamlet		374	163
–	–	–	–	–	–	–	–	–	–	–	–	–	–	–	–	–	–	1	–	–	–	(1)	–	–	–	–	–	–	Hamlet		373	165
–	–	–	–	–	1	–	–	–	–	–	–	–	–	–	–	–	–	–	–	–	–	(1)	1	–	–	–	–	–	Hamlet		370	168
–	–	–	–	–	–	–	–	–	–	–	–	–	–	–	–	–	–	–	–	–	–	(1)	1	–	–	–	–	–	Hamlet		370	169
–	–	–	–	–	–	–	–	–	–	–	–	–	–	–	–	–	–	–	–	–	–	(1)	1	–	–	–	–	–	Hamlet		366	171
–	–	–	–	–	1	–	–	1	–	–	–	–	–	–	–	–	1	–	–	–	–	(1)	1	–	–	–	–	–	Hamlet		359	176
–	–	–	–	–	–	–	–	–	–	–	–	–	–	–	–	–	–	–	–	–	–	(1)	1	–	–	–	–	–	Hamlet		357	177
–	–	–	–	–	–	–	–	–	–	–	–	–	–	–	–	–	–	–	–	–	–	–	–	–	–	–	–	–	Hamlet		340	186
–	–	–	–	–	–	–	–	–	–	–	–	–	–	–	–	–	–	–	–	–	–	(1)	–	–	–	–	–	–	Hamlet		335	192

Settlements	Antique shop	Bakers	Bicycle shops	Books and stationery	Butchers	Cafés	Car sales	Chemists	Clothes (general)	Clothes (ladies)	Clothes (men)	Sweets/tobacco	Electrical	Electrical showroom	Fancy goods	Fried fish	Fresh fish	Furniture stores	Garden supplies	Gas showroom	General stores	Greengrocer	Grocer	Hardware	Jeweller	Leather goods stores	Newsagents	Off Licences	Pet shops	Photographic supplies	Public Houses	Record shops	Restaurants	Shoe shops	Sports shops
Thompson	-	-	-	-	-	-	-	-	-	-	-	-	-	-	-	-	-	-	-	-	1	-	-	-	-	-	-	-	-	-	1	-	-	-	-
Ingham	-	-	-	-	-	-	-	-	-	-	-	-	-	-	-	-	-	-	-	-	1	-	1	-	-	-	-	-	-	-	1	-	-	-	-
Burrough Green	-	-	-	-	-	-	-	-	-	-	-	-	-	-	-	-	-	-	-	-	1	-	-	-	-	-	-	-	-	-	1	-	-	-	-
Hargrave	-	-	-	-	-	-	-	-	-	-	-	-	-	-	-	-	-	-	-	-	1	-	-	-	-	-	-	-	-	-	1	-	-	-	-
Herringswell	-	-	-	-	-	-	-	-	-	-	-	-	-	-	-	-	-	-	-	-	1	-	-	-	-	-	-	-	-	-	-	-	-	-	-
Cowlinge	-	-	-	-	-	-	-	-	-	-	-	-	-	-	-	-	-	-	-	-	1	-	-	-	-	-	-	-	-	-	1	-	-	-	-
Santon Downham	-	-	-	-	-	-	-	-	-	-	-	-	-	-	-	-	-	-	-	-	-	1	-	-	-	-	-	-	-	-	-	-	-	-	-
Eriswell	-	-	-	-	-	-	-	-	-	-	-	-	-	-	-	-	-	-	-	-	1	-	-	-	-	-	-	-	-	-	-	-	-	-	-
Hawstead	-	-	-	-	-	-	-	-	-	-	-	-	-	-	-	-	-	-	-	-	1	-	-	-	-	-	-	-	-	-	1	-	-	-	-
Foulden	-	-	-	-	-	-	-	-	-	-	-	-	-	-	-	-	-	-	-	-	1	-	-	-	-	-	-	-	-	-	1	-	-	-	-
Croxton	-	-	-	-	-	-	-	-	-	-	-	-	-	-	-	-	-	-	-	-	-	1	-	-	-	-	-	-	-	-	1	-	-	-	-
Dalham	-	-	-	-	-	-	-	-	-	-	-	-	-	-	-	-	-	-	-	-	1	-	-	-	-	-	-	-	-	-	1	-	-	-	-
Kentford	-	-	-	-	-	-	-	-	-	-	-	-	-	-	-	-	-	-	-	-	2	-	1	-	-	-	-	-	-	-	1	-	-	-	-
Lidgate	-	-	-	-	-	-	-	-	-	-	-	-	-	-	-	-	-	-	-	-	1	-	-	-	-	-	-	-	-	-	1	-	-	-	-
Chedburgh	-	-	-	-	-	-	-	-	-	-	-	-	-	-	-	-	-	-	-	-	-	1	-	-	-	-	-	-	-	-	1	-	-	-	-
Snailwell	-	-	-	-	-	-	-	-	-	-	-	-	-	-	-	-	-	-	-	-	1	-	-	-	-	-	-	-	-	-	1	-	-	-	-
Euston	-	-	-	-	-	-	-	-	-	-	-	-	-	-	-	-	-	-	-	-	1	-	-	-	-	-	-	-	-	-	-	-	-	-	-
Ousden	-	-	-	-	-	-	-	-	-	-	-	-	-	-	-	-	-	-	-	-	1	-	-	-	-	-	-	-	-	-	1	-	-	-	-
Stanningfield	-	-	-	-	-	-	-	-	-	-	-	-	-	-	-	-	-	-	-	-	1	-	-	-	-	-	-	-	-	-	1	-	-	-	-
Great Livermere	-	-	-	-	-	-	-	-	-	-	-	-	-	-	-	-	-	-	-	-	1	-	-	-	-	-	-	-	-	-	-	-	-	-	-
Higham	-	-	-	-	-	-	-	-	-	-	-	-	-	-	-	-	-	-	-	-	1	-	-	-	-	-	-	-	-	-	1	-	-	-	-
Cavenham	-	-	-	-	-	-	-	-	-	-	-	-	-	-	-	-	-	-	-	-	1	-	-	-	-	-	-	-	-	-	1	-	-	-	-
Great Saxham	-	-	-	-	-	-	-	-	-	-	-	-	-	-	-	-	-	-	-	-	-	-	-	-	-	-	-	-	-	-	-	-	-	-	-
Hengrave	-	-	-	-	-	-	-	-	-	-	-	-	-	-	-	-	-	-	-	-	-	-	-	-	-	-	-	-	-	-	-	-	-	-	-
Nowton	-	-	-	-	-	-	-	-	-	-	-	-	-	-	-	-	-	-	-	-	-	-	-	-	-	-	-	-	-	-	-	-	-	-	-
Westley Waterless	-	-	-	-	-	-	-	-	-	-	-	-	-	-	-	-	-	-	-	-	1	-	-	-	-	-	-	-	-	-	1	-	-	-	-
Flempton	-	-	-	-	-	-	-	-	-	-	1	-	-	-	-	-	-	-	-	-	-	-	-	-	-	-	-	-	-	-	1	-	-	-	-
Merton	-	-	-	-	-	-	-	-	-	-	-	-	-	-	-	-	-	-	-	-	-	-	-	-	-	-	-	-	-	-	-	-	-	-	-
Lackford	-	-	-	-	-	-	-	-	-	-	-	-	-	-	-	-	-	-	-	-	-	-	-	-	-	-	-	-	-	-	-	-	-	-	-
Ickburgh	-	-	-	-	-	-	-	-	-	-	-	-	-	-	-	-	-	-	-	-	1	-	-	-	-	-	-	-	-	-	-	-	-	-	-
Rede	-	-	-	-	-	-	-	-	-	-	-	-	-	-	-	-	-	-	-	-	-	-	-	-	-	-	-	-	-	-	-	-	-	-	-
Little Welnetham	-	-	-	-	-	-	-	-	-	-	-	-	-	-	-	-	-	-	-	-	-	-	-	-	-	-	-	-	-	-	-	-	-	-	-
Bradfield Combust	-	-	-	-	-	-	-	-	-	-	-	-	-	-	-	-	-	-	-	-	-	-	-	-	-	-	-	-	-	-	1	-	-	-	-
Little Saxham	-	-	-	-	-	-	-	-	-	-	-	-	-	-	-	-	-	-	-	-	-	-	-	-	-	-	-	-	-	-	-	-	-	-	-
Ampton	-	-	-	-	-	-	-	-	-	-	-	-	-	-	-	-	-	-	-	-	-	-	-	-	-	-	-	-	-	-	-	-	-	-	-
Kilverstone	-	-	-	-	-	-	-	-	-	-	-	-	-	-	-	-	-	-	-	-	-	-	-	-	-	-	-	-	-	-	-	-	-	-	-
Timworth	-	-	-	-	-	-	-	-	-	-	-	-	-	-	-	-	-	-	-	-	-	-	-	-	-	-	-	-	-	-	-	-	-	-	-
Westley	-	-	-	-	-	-	-	-	-	-	-	-	-	-	-	-	-	-	-	-	-	-	-	-	-	-	-	-	-	-	-	-	-	-	-
Rushbrooke	-	-	-	-	-	-	-	-	-	-	-	-	-	-	-	-	-	-	-	-	-	-	-	-	-	-	-	-	-	-	-	-	-	-	-
Didlington	-	-	-	-	-	-	-	-	-	-	-	-	-	-	-	-	-	-	-	-	-	-	-	-	-	-	-	-	-	-	-	-	-	-	-
Wangford	-	-	-	-	-	-	-	-	-	-	-	-	-	-	-	-	-	-	-	-	-	-	-	-	-	-	-	-	-	-	-	-	-	-	-
Cranwich	-	-	-	-	-	-	-	-	-	-	-	-	-	-	-	-	-	-	-	-	-	-	-	-	-	-	-	-	-	-	-	-	-	-	-
Wordwell	-	-	-	-	-	-	-	-	-	-	-	-	-	-	-	-	-	-	-	-	-	-	-	-	-	-	-	-	-	-	-	-	-	-	-

Do-it-yourself etc.	Woollens	Supermarket	Boots (Chemist)	Co-op department stores	Co-op grocers	Marks and Spencer	Woolworths	Petrol sales	Dry cleaners	Gents hairdressing	Ladies hairdressing	Launderettes	Photo studios	Shoe repairs	Banks	Betting shops	Cinemas	Garages	Hospitals	Hotels	Newspaper office	Post Offices	Primary schools	Secondary schools	Estate agents	Insurance offices	Opticians	Solicitors	Class according to the rank-size graphs	Class according to functions possessed	Population 1961	Rank in Norwich area
–	–	–	–	–	–	–	–	–	–	–	–	–	–	–	–	–	–	–	–	–	–	(1)	1	–	–	–	–	–	Hamlet		306	209
–	–	–	–	–	–	–	–	1	–	–	–	–	–	–	–	–	–	–	–	–	–	(1)	–	–	–	–	–	–	Hamlet		291	214
–	–	–	–	–	–	–	–	–	–	–	–	–	–	–	–	–	–	–	–	–	–	(1)	1	–	–	–	–	–	Hamlet		289	215
–	–	–	–	–	–	–	–	–	–	–	–	–	–	–	–	–	–	–	–	–	–	(1)	–	–	–	–	–	–	Hamlet		288	218
–	–	–	–	–	–	–	–	–	–	–	–	–	–	–	–	–	–	–	–	–	–	(1)	–	–	–	–	–	–	Hamlet		273	225
–	–	–	–	–	–	–	–	–	–	–	–	–	–	–	–	–	–	–	–	–	–	(1)	–	–	–	–	–	–	Hamlet		270	228
–	–	–	–	–	–	–	–	–	–	–	–	–	–	–	–	–	–	–	–	–	–	(1)	–	–	–	–	–	–	Hamlet		269	230
–	–	–	–	–	–	–	–	–	–	–	–	–	–	–	–	–	–	–	–	–	–	(1)	1	–	–	–	–	–	Hamlet		262	233
–	–	–	–	–	–	–	–	–	–	–	–	–	–	–	–	–	–	–	–	–	–	(1)	–	–	–	–	–	–	Hamlet		248	244
–	–	–	–	–	–	–	–	–	–	–	–	–	–	–	–	–	–	–	–	–	–	(1)	1	–	–	–	–	–	Hamlet		246	245
–	–	–	–	–	–	–	–	–	–	–	–	–	–	–	–	–	–	–	–	–	–	(1)	–	–	–	–	–	–	Hamlet		245	246
–	–	–	–	–	–	–	–	–	–	–	–	–	–	–	–	–	–	–	–	–	–	(1)	–	–	–	–	–	–	Hamlet		237	251
–	–	–	–	–	–	–	–	–	1	–	–	–	–	–	–	–	–	–	–	–	–	(1)	1	–	–	–	–	–	Hamlet		235	252
–	–	–	–	–	–	–	–	1	–	–	–	–	–	–	–	–	–	–	–	–	–	(1)	–	–	–	–	–	–	Hamlet		227	259
–	–	–	–	–	–	–	–	–	–	–	–	–	–	–	–	–	–	–	–	–	–	–	1	–	–	–	–	–	Hamlet		218	260
–	–	–	–	–	–	–	–	–	–	–	–	–	–	–	–	–	–	–	–	–	–	(1)	–	–	–	–	–	–	Hamlet		216	263
–	–	–	–	–	–	–	–	–	–	–	–	–	–	–	–	–	–	–	–	–	–	(1)	–	–	–	–	–	–	Hamlet		214	265
–	–	–	–	–	–	–	–	1	–	–	–	–	–	–	–	–	–	–	–	–	–	(1)	1	–	–	–	–	–	Hamlet		213	267
–	–	–	–	–	–	–	–	–	–	–	–	–	–	–	–	–	–	–	–	–	–	(1)	–	–	–	–	–	–	Hamlet		211	269
–	–	–	–	–	–	–	–	–	–	–	–	–	–	–	–	–	–	–	–	–	–	(1)	–	–	–	–	–	–	Hamlet		207	272
–	–	–	–	–	–	–	–	–	–	–	–	–	–	–	–	–	–	–	–	–	–	(1)	1	–	–	–	–	–	Hamlet		205	273
–	–	–	–	–	–	–	–	–	–	–	–	–	–	–	–	–	–	–	–	–	–	(1)	1	–	–	–	–	–	Hamlet		200	276
–	–	–	–	–	–	–	–	–	–	–	–	–	–	–	–	–	–	–	–	–	–	–	–	–	–	–	–	–	Hamlet		189	280
–	–	–	–	–	–	–	–	–	–	–	–	–	–	–	–	–	–	–	–	–	–	–	–	–	–	–	–	–	Hamlet		188	281
–	–	–	–	–	–	–	–	–	–	–	–	–	–	–	–	–	–	–	–	–	–	–	–	–	–	–	–	–	Hamlet		184	284
–	–	–	–	–	–	–	–	–	–	–	–	–	–	–	–	–	–	–	–	–	–	(1)	1	–	–	–	–	–	Hamlet		155	298
–	–	–	–	–	–	–	–	–	–	–	–	–	–	–	–	–	–	–	–	–	–	(1)	1	–	–	–	–	–	Hamlet		151	300
–	–	–	–	–	–	–	–	–	–	–	–	–	–	–	–	–	–	–	–	–	–	–	–	–	–	–	–	–	Hamlet		149	301
–	–	–	–	–	–	–	–	–	–	–	–	–	–	–	–	–	–	–	–	–	–	–	–	–	–	–	–	–	Hamlet		146	304
–	–	–	–	–	–	–	–	–	–	–	–	–	–	–	–	–	–	–	–	–	–	–	–	–	–	–	–	–	Hamlet		141	310
–	–	–	–	–	–	–	–	–	–	–	–	–	–	–	–	–	–	–	–	–	–	–	–	–	–	–	–	–	Hamlet		136	314
–	–	–	–	–	–	–	–	–	–	–	–	–	–	–	–	–	–	–	–	–	–	–	–	–	–	–	–	–	Hamlet		111	322
–	–	–	–	–	–	–	–	–	–	–	–	–	–	–	–	–	–	–	–	–	–	–	–	–	–	–	–	–	Hamlet		108	323
–	–	–	–	–	–	–	–	–	–	–	–	–	–	–	–	–	–	–	–	–	–	–	–	–	–	–	–	–	Hamlet		92	331
–	–	–	–	–	–	–	–	–	–	–	–	–	–	–	–	–	–	–	–	–	–	–	–	–	–	–	–	–	Hamlet		89	332
–	–	–	–	–	–	–	–	–	–	–	–	–	–	–	–	–	–	–	–	–	–	–	–	–	–	–	–	–	Hamlet		84	334
–	–	–	–	–	–	–	–	–	–	–	–	–	–	–	–	–	–	–	–	–	–	–	–	–	–	–	–	–	Hamlet		69	342
–	–	–	–	–	–	–	–	–	–	–	–	–	–	–	–	–	–	–	–	–	–	–	–	–	–	–	–	–	Hamlet		61	346
–	–	–	–	–	–	–	–	–	–	–	–	–	–	–	–	–	–	–	–	–	–	–	–	–	–	–	–	–	Hamlet		58	347
–	–	–	–	–	–	–	–	–	–	–	–	–	–	–	–	–	–	–	–	–	–	–	–	–	–	–	–	–	Hamlet		53	349
–	–	–	–	–	–	–	–	–	–	–	–	–	–	–	–	–	–	–	–	–	–	–	–	–	–	–	–	–	Hamlet		36	355
–	–	–	–	–	–	–	–	–	–	–	–	–	–	–	–	–	–	–	–	–	–	–	–	–	–	–	–	–	Hamlet		35	356
–	–	–	–	–	–	–	–	–	–	–	–	–	–	–	–	–	–	–	–	–	–	–	–	–	–	–	–	–	Hamlet		30	357

Note : Post Offices are marked (1) if they are found in association with another function

expect to find respectively in a hamlet, a village, a town, and a city, of the type that has been discussed.

Figure 46 lists those functions which *we* would expect to indicate hamlet, village, town and city status. This list is by no means comprehensive, and many functions have been omitted. At this stage it would be interesting to compare your list with ours, realising, of course, that no firm rules are possible, and that there are bound to be discrepancies between actual settlements.

From an examination of fig. 46 it can be seen that as a progression is made from lower order settlements (hamlets and villages) to those of higher order (towns and cities) lower order functions or convenience goods such as groceries or newspapers are repeated. The higher order functions, supplying shopping and specialist goods such as furniture and jewellery and higher order services, such as banking and specialised entertainments, are added to the town and city settlements. These higher order functions require a greater population for their support, and this has to be attracted from a larger area. Thus the range of these goods and services is greater than those of a lower order.

As can be seen from fig. 46, and indeed from your own experience, not only do more specialised functions appear with increasing status of settlement, but also shops supplying certain types of goods or services themselves become more specialised. For example, in towns one may find continental food stores in addition to the more usual grocers, and fashion houses in cities as well as the more typical clothes shops of the town.

Now turning to a part of the actual study-area, fig. 47 shows all the settlements ranked according to population, with almost all the functions that they possess listed. There is an expected progression in the possession of functions as larger settlements are reached. However, there are some marked discrepancies, the reasons for which we might consider a little later. As already implied, it should be possible to classify the settlements according to functional content. Many functions show a very irregular distribution and would therefore be very poor indicators of status. These functions are more usually geared, say, to the whims of the passing motorist (for example, the wayside café or service station) and may be more dependent upon the presence of important highways than the interaction between local consumer and local service centre. With the advent of the motor car such developments are becoming increasingly important; this is especially to be seen in the United States of America, where considerable developments have taken place in ribbon form along main highways, often many miles from older established centres. Despite these and other problems, it is perhaps possible to select certain functions as being indicators of settlement status.

Fig. 48 Functions selected as indicators of settlement status in the hierarchy of hamlet/village/town/city

Hamlet	*Village*	*Town*	*City*
General stores plus Grocers	Butcher	Clothes store	Hospital
Public House	**Hardware/ Appliance**	Hairdresser (gents)	Cathedral
Post Office		Secondary School	University
Primary School		**Shoe shop**	
		Bank	
		Supermarket or Department Store	

Figure 48 lists those functions which have been selected as possible indicators because of their apparently regular distribution. Note that none of the indicators taken on their own would define the status of a settlement, and, indeed, it is likely that any one settlement of a certain status will not have all the indicators suggested. This applies particularly at the city end of the classification hierarchy. Here the indicators point to a high regional influence, a regional centre for education, government, entertainment, and religion, apart from the supply of very specialised goods.

In fig. 49 these special indicators have been placed on a simple matrix type diagram, and using the information suggested by fig. 48 the four main settlement categories have been blocked off according to the functions selected as indicators. This gives an easily comprehended view of

Fig. 49 Expected indicator functions according to class of settlement

	General Stores + Grocers	Public House	**Post Office**	Primary School	Butcher	**Hardware/ Appliances**	Clothes store	Hairdresser (gents)	Secondary School	**Shoe shop**	Bank	Supermarket or Dept. Store	Hospital	Cathedral	University
Hamlet	X	X	X	X											
Village	X	X	X	X	X	X									
Town	X	X	X	X	X	X	X	X	X	X	X	X			
City	X	X	X	X	X	X	X	X	X	X	X	X	X	X	X

what the expected class of settlement would contain in the way of indicator functions.

Refer again to fig. 47 which shows the data collected for a relatively small part of the total area. Consider also the map fig. 31 facing page 45 where it can be seen that this area lies to the south-west of Thetford. Here the settlements are again ranked by population, together with an indication of the classification that was applied on the grounds of size. The bold type in the columns headed Post Office, Hardware and Shoes, indicate the separations between classes of settlement shown on fig. 49. What can you suggest about the relative efficiency of the boundaries separating settlement categories obtained by these indicators ? Remember that the best classification is one which minimises the differences within the classes, and maximises the differences between them. Which is the most significant class boundary ?

The use of hardware as an indicator of village rather than town status may be considered to be of doubtful validity. Two points arise. One is that most village stores sell hardware of a limited range as a significant part of their goods; the lack of hardware stores in villages may be attributable to this. The second point is that hardware goods in specialised hardware stores (as opposed to village general stores) are usually a mixture of the so-called convenience goods and shopping goods. Thus the presence or absence of stores retailing shopping goods (e.g. clothes, shoes, sports articles, etc.) would appear to be very critical in the separation of towns from villages. The problems associated with the use of

Fig. 50 Numbers of certain functions found in the larger settlements of the Norwich area

Settlement	Population	1	2	3	4	5	6	7	8	9	10	11
Norwich	120,096	30	80	33	160	2	22	16	1	1	2	13
Kings Lynn	27,536	7	16	7	22	1	6	5	1	0	1	5
Bury	21,179	8	16	5	26	1	8	2	1	1	1	6
Newmarket	11,227	1	7	2	13	1	3	1	0	0	1	2
Hellesdon	9,744	0	0	0	0	0	1	1	0	0	0	0
Stowmarket	7,795	1	3	4	17	1	3	3	0	0	1	2
East Dereham	7,199	3	3	4	15	1	3	2	0	0	0	1
Mildenhall	7,132	1	1	1	4	0	1	0	0	0	1	2
Costessey	7,051	0	0	0	0	0	1	0	0	0	0	0
Wymondham	5,904	0	2	2	2	0	3	1	0	0	1	1
Thetford	5,399	3	4	3	3	0	3	3	0	0	1	0
Lakenheath	4,512	0	0	1	0	0	0	0	0	0	0	0
Diss	3,681	2	3	4	11	0	4	0	0	0	0	3
Brandon	3,341	0	0	1	2	0	1	0	0	0	0	0

Settlement	Population	1	2	3	4	5	6	7	8	9	10	11
Swaffham	3,202	1	1	2	6	0	2	2	0	0	0	0
Feltwell	3,192	0	0	1	0	0	0	0	0	0	0	0
Attleborough	3,027	0	2	2	3	0	1	1	0	0	0	1
Marham	3,021	0	0	0	0	0	0	0	0	0	0	0
Downham	2,835	2	4	4	6	0	3	1	0	0	0	1
Catton	2,592	0	0	0	0	0	1	0	0	0	0	0
Watton	2,462	1	0	2	6	0	1	0	0	0	0	1
Harleston	1,809	0	0	0	0	0	0	0	0	0	0	0
Swanton Morley	1,775	0	0	0	0	0	0	0	0	0	0	0
Fordham	1,709	0	0	0	0	0	0	0	0	0	0	0
Needham Market	1,674	0	0	1	7	0	0	0	0	0	0	0
Cheveley	1,624	0	0	0	0	0	0	0	0	0	0	0
Hethersett	1,613	0	0	0	0	0	0	0	0	0	0	0
Eye	1,583	1	1	2	5	0	1	0	0	0	0	0
Methwold	1,560	0	0	0	0	0	1	0	0	0	0	0
Honington	1,546	0	0	0	0	0	0	0	0	0	0	0
Isleham	1,392	0	0	0	0	0	0	0	0	0	0	0
Hingham	1,388	0	0	1	0	0	0	0	0	0	0	0
Horsham	1,361	0	0	0	0	0	0	0	0	0	0	0
Drayton	1,346	0	0	0	0	0	0	0	0	0	0	0
Hilgay	1,343	0	0	0	0	0	0	0	0	0	0	0
Reepham	1,276	0	0	1	2	0	1	1	0	0	0	0
Stanton	1,252	0	0	0	0	0	0	0	0	0	0	0
Shipdham	1,237	0	0	0	0	0	0	0	0	0	0	0
Taverham	1,219	0	0	0	0	0	0	0	0	0	0	0
Carbrooke	1,215	0	0	0	0	0	0	0	0	0	0	0
Southery	1,209	0	0	1	0	0	0	0	0	0	0	0
Elmswell	1,177	0	0	0	0	0	0	0	0	0	0	0

Minimum threshold

Average minimum threshold

Average for Norwich

Key: *1* accountants, *2* dentists, *3* banks, *4* solicitors, *5* Boots (chemist), *6* secondary school,
7 Hospitals, *8* Marks and Spencers, *9* Sainsburys, *10* Woolworths, *11* auctioneers and estate agents
Sources: *The Dentists' Register*, 1966; *Education Authorities Directory and Annual*, 1966; *Law List*, 1966;
Hospitals' Year Book, 1967

'village' indicators, and the very blurred distinction between villages and hamlets suggests that between these two classes there is a continuous variation and little break. Hence it may be more convenient, in this area at least, to classify them as one.

Figure 50 gives the population for the city of Norwich together with the towns and larger villages of the area. Selected services are included and the presence of certain large chain stores has also been indicated. From the table state at which size of settlement each function or store appears. This can be called the minimum threshold value of the function.

However such a settlement often stands on its own in possessing a particular function or store which may be lacking in larger settlements. Thus to discover what minimum population is required by a settlement to support a certain function precautions have to be taken against the anomalous example. To make allowance for this, it is suggested that the population of the settlements concerned be totalled from that settlement where the function first appears, to the settlement one above the largest without that particular function but only totalling the population figures of the settlements which possess the function. This figure should be divided by the total number of this function that these settlements possess. For example, in the case of Woolworths, the first settlement with that particular service is Thetford, with a population of 5,399. This could be considered as the minimum threshold value for that function in this particular group of settlements. However, the average value as calculated above for the support of one of these functions is 7,491. This, then, appears to be approximately the value necessary for the support of this particular function, at least in this area. This value indicates the approximate size that a settlement has to be before the entry of any particular function. After all an entrepreneur, if he has made a rational decision, will require a certain minimum potential market to make a satisfactory living. As the population size of the settlement increases, so the potential market increases, and the more attractive the settlement becomes for a second entrepreneur in competition with the first. It is interesting to compare the two values we have arrived at for the threshold value with the share each function has in a large town or city. In the case of Woolworths, the average threshold value of 7,491 is not well matched by an average share of 60,048 in the case of Norwich. Can you suggest reasons for this apparent anomaly? Perhaps shop-floor areas should have been taken into account. Would the population size of the catchment areas of the settlements make any difference?

In all cases of personal services, such as solicitors, accountants, etc., there always seem to be one or two who have located in surprisingly small settlements. The same can be said for some other functions, such as banks, hospitals and certain schools. In the case of solicitors and accountants, this can easily be accounted for by the mobility which the car gives to the professional man and his clients. Thus he is free to locate his offices in more attractive areas than the larger towns provide, where not only is there the discomfort and inconvenience attributed by some to living in towns, but also the higher rents, rates, etc. These factors have to be weighed against proximity to clients, many of whom would be city firms, but newer entries to the profession do not necessarily have these ties and are free to locate according to personal whims.

The same kinds of arguments can be applied to other apparent anomalies. What reasons can you give concerning the location of certain banks in small settlements? Would these necessarily be open all the week? If not, why not? What factors might cause the location of schools and hospitals near small villages or indeed, away from settlements altogether? What kinds of shops may decide to locate away from the size of settlement that they might be expected to require for their support? What does this suggest about their type of goods, or about the mobility of their customers? Could a decision to locate in a below-threshold settlement be accounted for by any other factors such as poor locational knowledge on the part of the entrepreneur who is perhaps a villager?

There are many examples of poor decisions concerning the location of shop types. You may be able to think of examples. What factors may indicate this to an observant geographer? How can poor locations be viable, particularly where a family unit is concerned? What state of affairs would there be if the family's time spent in the shop were properly costed?

To return to the matter of threshold values. Work out, in small groups, the threshold values for each of the functions listed in fig. 50. Figure 47 for a smaller area may also be used. Again anomalies will be apparent. Where possible attempt to put forward possible explanations for these. For information, fig. 51 indicates the estimated population requirements of several well-known firms.

Fig. 51 Estimated population requirements of several well-known firms

Boots the Chemists	10,000
Mac Fisheries	25,000
Barratts	20,000–30,000
Sainsbury	60,000 (for a medium-sized self-service store)
Marks and Spencer	50,000–100,000
John Lewis	50,000 (a supermarket)
John Lewis	100,000 (a department store)

Source: M. Collins, *Field Work in Urban Areas* (Chorley and Haggett, 1965, p. 227)

From the type of work we have considered it is, perhaps, possible to classify settlements into a hierarchy according to functional content. Refer now to fig. 47 and complete the column on the status of settlement according to function. How does this vary with the hierarchical classification according to population size? Try to account for any anomalies. Use the location map (fig. 31) to help you.

Figure 52 gives a comparison of the ideas of a number of geographers

Fig. 52 A hierarchy of central places (adapted from H. Carol, *The IGU Symposium in Urban Geography* pp. 558–559)

General hierarchy	Special hierarchies for the highest level of central function				
	Entire settlements			Centres within a city	
	Christaller (Germany)	*G.B. scale*	*Switzerland scale*	*Scale for Zürich centres*	*Scale for G.B. centres*
First Lowest		Roadside hamlet (Chippenham)	Dorf	Local business district	Local centre
Second Low order	Marktort	Village (Old Buckenham)	Marktort	Neighbourhood business district	Neighbourhood centre
Third Middle order	Amtsort Kreisort Beziksort	Town (Thetford)	Stadt	Regional business district	Community centre
Fourth High order	Gauort Provinzhauptort	City (Norwich)	Grossstadt		Regional centre
Fifth Higher order	Landstadt	Metropolis (Bristol)	Metropole	Central business district	Metropolitan centre
Sixth Highest order	Reichsteile	Super Metropolis (Manchester)			Super metropolitan centre
Seventh World wide order	Reichstadt	World metropolitan centre (London)			

concerning the naming of the hierarchy of settlements. It suggests that a hierarchy of shopping districts may also exist within a city. This point will be expanded in Book 2.

The problems of hierarchy and threshold values have been extensively discussed and written about in recent years. Bracey's work on villages in Somerset is important as is the work of Berry and Garrison in the United States on the threshold value. An examination of these articles could suggest work that you might like to carry out on your own or as a group. However the work done by Berry and Garrison has been criticised by W. Bunge in *Theoretical Geography* 1966, pp. 149–50, and his words are worth quoting here, in view of the work we have already carried out.

One of Christaller's fundamental assumptions was that some lower limit of number of consumers was required before a given type of function could come into existence. This lower limit has since come to be known as the 'threshold' size. Some experimental work has been done on threshold sizes. The economist Bain has attempted to measure the thresholds of large or medium sized activities. Berry and Garrison have attempted to study thresholds of small activities. However, their work is not actually concerned with thresholds for they do not deal with the total number of consumers necessary for the existence of an activity, but rather with the population of the centre where these activities appear. They ignore rural and highway consumers which contribute to the geometric drop of the number of people per activity in small towns where the rural and highway users make up a large percentage of consumers. Similar largely inadequate studies of small centres have been made by rural sociologists and others.

Perhaps this view may help to explain some of the anomalies noted. In considering the tables given in fig. 50 and fig. 32 the settlements of Hellesdon, Costessey, Marham, Catton and Harleston stand out in two ways. First, they have fewer functions than would be expected in a centre of their size and secondly they have all grown very rapidly in the years between 1921 and 1961. Two answers to this problem can be considered. In fig. 53 the 'normal' relationship of increasing numbers of goods as the population size grows is seen in the middle of the graph (group A). Above these lie a number of settlements (group B) which possess more functions than their size seems to warrant. Berry describes these settlements as resorts which gain their extra functions by serving tourists as well as their normal populations. How would you describe the settlements in group C which correspond to the settlements named earlier? They can be described as 'dormitory' settlements. Ones that have grown up around a large city, in this case Norwich, which completes the range

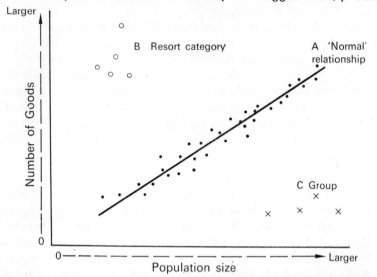

Fig. 53 Simplified relationship of numbers of functions to size of settlement (after B. J. Garner in Chorley and Haggett 1968, p. 323)

of functions needed by this suburban fringe. A second explanation is possible in some cases. New housing has been provided in certain areas for the civilians and servicemen working in the many British and American air bases which are found in East Anglia. Many of the goods required by these shoppers are provided by the local NAAFI or PX stores and not by the settlement. Both explanations account for the recent sharp increase in population shown in the census returns.

Read

BERRY, B. J. L. and GARRISON, W. L. 'A note on central place theory and the range of a good', *Economic Geography*, vol. 34, 1958, pp. 304–311.

BERRY, B. J. L. and GARRISON, W. L. 'Functional bases of the central place hierarchy', *Economic Geography*, vol. 34, 1958, pp. 145–54.

BRACEY, H. E. 'English central villages: identification, distribution and functions', *I.G.U. Symposium in Urban Geography*, pp. 169–90.

GARNER, B. J. 'Models of Urban Geography and Settlement Location' in R. J. Chorley and P. Haggett, *Socio-Economic Models in Geography*, pp. 322–326.

Further reading

BUNGE, W. *Theoretical Geography*, 2nd edn, Lund, Studies in Geography, series C, 1966, pp. 149–50.

HAGGETT, P. *Locational Analysis in Human Geography*, pp. 114–18.

8 The interaction of fields of influence

In chapter 7 it was shown that there appeared to be a characteristic assemblage of functions associated with each size group of settlement, and that this also appeared to be associated with a hierarchy in the settlement pattern. In this manner all centres of a given order compete with each other (and with other centres of a higher order over their common range of functions) for the custom of their surrounding regions. The concept of a retail service field applies, of course, to two components of the population. On the one hand it applies to subsidiary settlements within the main settlement's sphere of influence, and on the other to the population of the main centre itself.

Fig. 54 Households and villages near Hartington in the Peak District

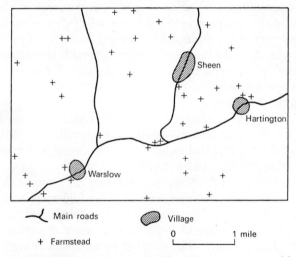

Between settlements of a given size and order, one would expect to find a boundary zone where allegiance to one or other of the two settlements is indeterminate. Such a zone is the boundary between each field of influence, and any point on it may be termed an 'interaction breaking point'.

Figure 54 shows an area in the Peak District of Derbyshire, between Buxton and Bakewell, where the results of a questionnaire survey showed that the households between the villages of Hartington, Sheen and

Fig. 55 Shopping allegiances at the grocery level

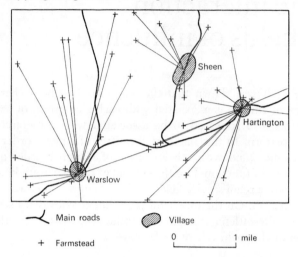

Warslow shared their shopping allegiances in the manner shown in fig. 55. This diagram indicates something of both the range of the good in question and the retail service fields of the villages concerned.

The discovery of the limits of the fields of influence of settlements at the various levels in the hierarchy is of considerable importance to town and regional planners, and the need for ease of determination has prompted the construction of a number of theoretical models based mainly on population size.

Figure 56 shows an enlarged part of the Norwich area. On it are marked a number of centres classified as towns, villages and hamlets on the basis of figures supplied in fig. 33. Using overlays of tracing paper construct what you would expect to be the retail service area boundaries for hamlets, villages and towns, assuming that the boundaries are equidistant between pairs of like settlements. (See folder opposite.)

It is held by most settlement geographers that the area of influence surrounding each of a pair of competing centres varies proportionately to the size of each centre. The simplest possibility is that the distance between two centres could be divided in the proportions of the size of the populations of the two centres. With reference to fig. 57 where two centres are shown of population 300 and 500 respectively located four miles apart, the 'breaking point' would be expected to lie at a distance of $2\frac{1}{2}$ miles from the larger centre, the intervening distance having been divided in the proportion 5 : 3.

This provides the simplest model, and may approach reality where the populations of competing centres are not very different. Try this model on fig. 56 using the same techniques as were used above. However, where the population of neighbouring pairs of centres varies considerably, this model tends to be inaccurate.

Fig. 57 'Breaking point' between two centres *i* and *j* of population 300 and 500 respectively, four miles apart

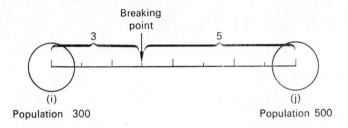

One of the most satisfactory models used to predict the size of fields of influence is one that has been borrowed from physical science, and as such is termed an 'analogue' model. This model uses the Newtonian theory of gravitation, and suggests that the movement between two centres is proportional to the products of their populations (in physics represented by mass), and inversely proportional to the square of the distance separating them. This can be formulated as

$$M_{ij} = \frac{P_i P_j}{(d_{ij})^2}$$

where M_{ij} is the interaction between two centres *i* and *j*, of population P_i and P_j respectively, and d_{ij} is the distance between them.

Fig. 58 Circulation of 'breaking point' using the gravity formula

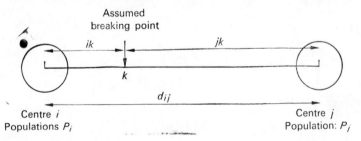

This formulation, developed as the *Law of Retail Gravitation* by W. J. Reilly of the University of Texas about 1930, can be used to find the interaction breaking point in the following manner: Examine fig. 58 which shows two settlements *i* and *j* of population P_i and P_j respectively, separated by a distance d_{ij}. Using the gravity model or inverse square law for the interaction (M_{ij}) between two settlements, we obtain:

$$M_{ij} = \frac{P_i P_j}{(d_{ij})^2}$$

In fig. 58 let k be the breaking point. Therefore the interaction between i and k will equal the interaction between k and j.

i.e. $M_{ik} = M_{jk}$

but $M_{ik} = \dfrac{P_i P_k}{(d_{ik})^2}$ and $M_{jk} = \dfrac{P_j P_k}{(d_{jk})^2}$

where d_{ik} and d_{jk} are the distances between i and k and j and k respectively.

Therefore:

$$\frac{P_i P_k}{(d_{ik})^2} = \frac{P_j P_k}{(d_{jk})^2} \quad (\text{as } M_{ik} = M_{jk})$$

therefore

$$P_i P_k (d_{jk})^2 = P_j P_k (d_{ik})^2 \quad (\text{by cross multiplication})$$

therefore

$$\frac{P_i P_k}{P_j P_k} = \frac{(d_{ik})^2}{(d_{jk})^2} \quad (\text{divide by } (d_{jk})^2 \text{ and divide by } P_j P_k)$$

therefore

$$\frac{P_i}{P_j} = \frac{(d_{ik})^2}{(d_{jk})^2}$$

therefore

$$\sqrt{\frac{P_i}{P_j}} = \frac{d_{ik}}{d_{jk}} \quad (\text{square root of both sides})$$

Now

$$1 + \sqrt{\frac{P_i}{P_j}} = 1 + \frac{d_{ik}}{d_{jk}} = \frac{d_{jk} + d_{ik}}{d_{jk}} = \frac{d_{ij}}{d_{jk}}$$

$$(\text{substituting } d_{ij} \text{ for } d_{jk} + d_{ik})$$

therefore

$$1 + \sqrt{\frac{P_i}{P_j}} = \frac{d_{ij}}{d_{jk}} \quad \text{or, by inverting,} \quad \frac{1}{1 + \sqrt{\dfrac{P_i}{P_j}}} = \frac{d_{jk}}{d_{ij}}$$

therefore

$$\frac{d_{ij}}{1 + \sqrt{\dfrac{P_i}{P_j}}} = d_{jk} \quad (\text{by multiplying by } d_{ij})$$

Thus

$$d_{jk} = \frac{d_{ij}}{1 + \sqrt{\dfrac{P_i}{P_j}}}$$

Fig. 59 Council Bluffs, Iowa—Farmers' preferences, 1934 : grocery shopping (after Berry 1967, p. 11)

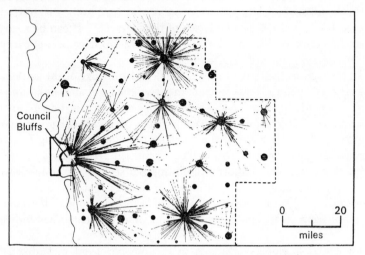

Thus in the case of the settlements of population 500 and 300, four miles apart, sited in fig. 57 above, this formula would predict a breaking point approximately 2·2 miles from the larger centre.

Making use of fig. 57 (population figures to be found in fig. 33), apply this formula to the settlements concerned, using tracing paper as suggested earlier.

Fig. 60 Council Bluffs, Iowa—Farmers' preferences, 1934 : lawyer's office location (after Berry 1967, p. 11)

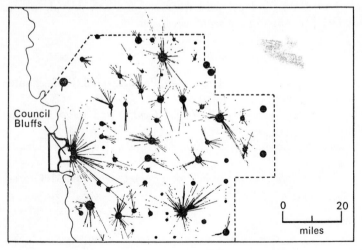

Examination of figs. 59 and 60 (taken from Professor B. J. L. Berry's book *The Geography of Market Centres and Retail Distribution*, chapter 1), show the form of settlement service areas in an area to the east of Council Bluffs, Iowa, in 1934, at two levels of the hierarchy. It can be seen that there is relatively little overlap (although overlap does occur) except in the peripheral 'zone of indifference'.

In the case of the gravity model the population size of the settlements has been taken as the mass element in Newton's Law, and the assumption has been made that the basic reason for the existence of the settlement is as a service centre. However with any two settlements of a given population size, the proportion of the working population working in a retail service capacity for the surrounding catchment area will vary considerably. If a town with a substantial industrial sector is examined, would the population size be the best indicator to use? It would be interesting to use other indicators such as numbers of 'shopping goods' shops in place of population in the gravity interaction model. What other indicators could be used?

Of course regional variations in income per head may distort the pattern, as will variations in population density within the spheres of influence. So too, lines of communication, the intervention of alternative centres (usually referred to as intervening opportunity), and varying friction of distance may cause the pattern to be distorted in size and shape. Variations in the friction of distance may involve changing technology (the advent of the car or of an efficient public transport system), or again variations in income which will in turn affect ability to travel to what would otherwise be preferred centres.

The gravity model for measuring the interaction between centres is an ideal medium for local field research, and can provide a suitable framework for individual research in the field.

Read

ALEXANDER, J. W. *Economic Geography*, Prentice-Hall, 1963, chapter 32: Location Theory, pp. 624–6.

BERRY, B. J. L., *Geography of Market Centers and Retail Distribution*, chapter 1.

HAGGETT, P., *Locational Analysis in Human Geography*, chapter 2, pp. 33–47.

MURPHY, R. E. *The American City: an Urban Geography*, McGraw-Hill, 1966, chapter 4.

9 The theoretical basis of central place

It would now be interesting to build up some form of predictive theory concerning the shape that these areas or fields of influence will take. In order to do this we turn our attention away from the study area and look at a hypothetical landscape.

We return to the time of the first settlement of such a hypothetical area, where we assume the newly settled population to be predominantly agricultural. We also assume that families tend to settle in groups, if only for the sake of companionship and defence against possible marauders. Thus small but largely self-sufficient hamlets are established, each with its group of families farming the land around it.

If it is assumed that the physical and farming characteristics of the area are everywhere the same, and that each settlement consisted of an equal number of farmers each gaining a sufficient livelihood from the

Fig. 61 Hamlets spaced two miles apart on an equilateral triangular grid

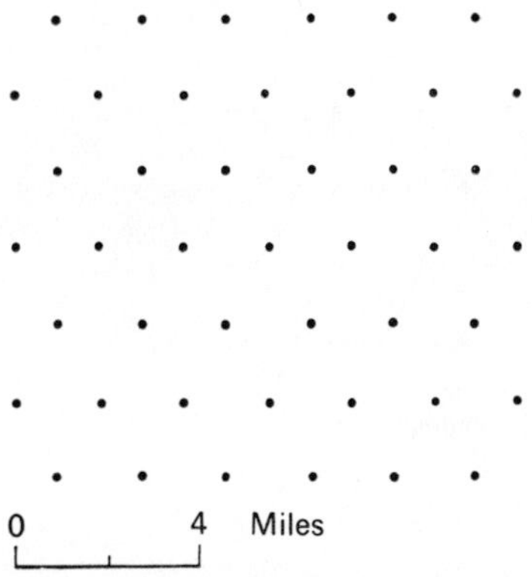

Fig. 62 Hamlets spaced two miles apart on a square grid

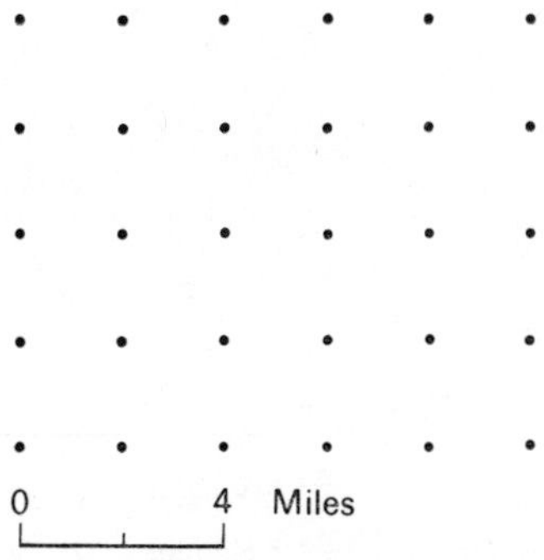

land, then the distribution of hamlets seen in fig. 61 will be expected. Here the pattern is perfectly regular, with each hamlet located at the apex of an equilateral triangle. In this case, the hamlets have been spaced at a distance of two miles from each other. Other factors being held constant, what factors would you expect to affect this spacing? Under what conditions would you expect the hamlets to be more closely packed?

A homogeneous environment such as the one described is usually referred to as an isotropic one.

Figure 62 shows the hypothetical situation where the hamlets are located at the vertices of squares with sides of length two miles. Suggest why such a pattern is less likely under isotropic conditions than that shown in fig. 61.

So far the hamlets have been assumed to be more or less self-sufficient. However as advances are made in technology through time, it is safe to predict that some specialisation of production will occur, and that given reasonable roads some trading will develop between centres. Therefore it would be expected that the occasional hamlet would contain an enterprising group of people who would see the advantages of organising the exchange, or buying and selling of local produce. By doing this the group concerned would make a little more profit than it would do otherwise. Now if it is assumed that a two-mile journey either way is the farthest that a farmer would be willing to travel on foot, it can be seen that the

Fig. 63 Pattern of hamlets and villages service area governed by a *k* = 3 hierarchy

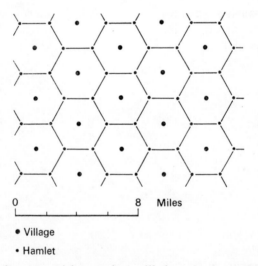

0   8   Miles

• Village

· Hamlet

hamlet with the enterprising traders will share in the trade of six of the surrounding hamlets, and of course, its own. The trading area (worked on the basis of a day's travel) of this central place hamlet is seen to be hexagonal in shape. Other centres are seen to develop in a similar manner, as profit is seen to be gained in acting as a trading centre. If the trade of the equivalent of three hamlets is required to make a reasonable profit for the trader, the form that the hexagons must take would be that shown in fig. 63. Here the hamlets around the central place hamlet each share their trade between three trading areas. Thus there are six one-third allegiances, and this added to the original hamlet makes a total custom of three.

At this point it is relevant to note that the hexagonal form of these service areas is mathematically the most efficient. This subject is often referred to as elementary packing theory. One can judge the efficiency of packed shapes in two ways. The first concerns the efficiency of movement, i.e. as measured by the distance from the centre to the most outlying parts of its boundary; and secondly by the efficiency of the shape's bounding limits, i.e. the measure of the length of the perimeter for a given area of territory. With a given unit of area, the circle is the most efficient from both these points of view. However, a circle as has been seen earlier is a shape that will not pack without leaving spaces between

Fig. 64 Efficiency of alternative types of regular polygons in relation to distance from centres and perimeter lengths (after P. Haggett, 1965)

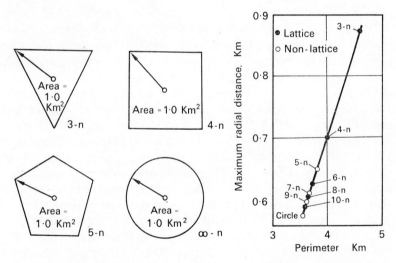

neighbouring circles. The only regular polygons that will allow packing (i.e. will allow the formation of regular lattices) are the triangle, the square and the hexagon. Given that the area of each of an equilateral triangle, a square, a regular hexagon and a circle is one square kilometre, fig. 64 shows the maximum radial distance in kilometres plotted against the length of perimeter in kilometres. From this it can be seen that of all the regular 'tessellations', the hexagon retains most of the advantages of the circle, being about four-fifths as efficient as the circle.

Walter Christaller, a German geographer, was the first to recognise this principle in 1933, and he found that the hexagonal lattices could be arranged in a number of ways. His theoretical model was described in what is now accepted as an important and influential book *Die Zentralen Orte in Suddeutschland,* which has recently been translated by C. W. Baskin as *Central Places in Southern Germany.*

Of Walter Christaller's work, William Bunge (*Theoretical Geography,* 1966, p. 133) has said:

> If it were not for the existence of central place theory, it would not be possible to be so emphatic about the existence of a theoretical geography independent of any set of mother sciences. Geography is a basic science since it produces new theory and the proof of that assertion lies most clearly in the existence of central place theory. With the possible exception of cartography, this author is of the opinion that the initial and growing beauty of central place theory is geography's finest intellectual product and puts Christaller in a place of great honor.

In his work Christaller relates the form of the service areas of settlements to their functional structure (through the supply of goods and services), building up a hierarchy of settlement and illustrating his theory from direct observation in south-west Germany.

Returning to the hypothetical landscape with its pattern of hamlets and central place hamlets, or villages, it can be seen that as more specialisation is achieved and as communication improves further, so the settlements will become less and less self-supporting. Several of the villages will specialise still further, introducing higher order goods and services for sale. These will not be required in such great quantities as the lower order goods and services (everyday requirements), and with their higher threshold values must draw upon much larger areas to produce a reasonable profit. If it is assumed that these market towns require a service area the equivalent in size of three whole village areas, then what pattern will emerge? Figure 65 shows the superimposition of the village fields of influence and those at the higher order market town level. Using this diagram measure the distances separating the villages and the market towns.

As has been seen in this example the total number of settlements of a certain order served by a central place of the next higher order is three. Christaller termed this the k value. In this case $k = 3$. In fig. 65 a $k = 3$ lattice is shown. However if the hexagonal net is turned through ninety

Fig. 65 Hamlets, villages and towns in a 'fixed-*k*' hierarchy where
k = 3 (Christaller's 'marketing' principle)

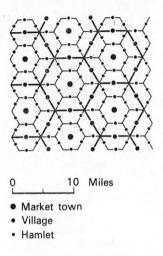

```
0            10   Miles
```

● Market town
• Village
· Hamlet

degrees, the border settlements will be shared by only two central places
and thus the *k* value rises to four, as is shown in fig. 66. Figure 67 shows
the process of net enlargement moving one step further to produce a

Fig. 66 Pattern of service areas of villages in a *k* = 4 hierarchy

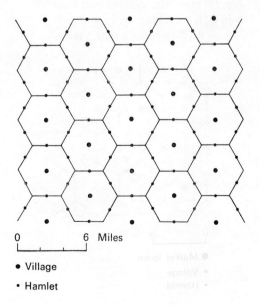

```
0         6   Miles
```

● Village
· Hamlet

Fig. 67 Pattern of service areas of villages in a *k* = 7 hierarchy

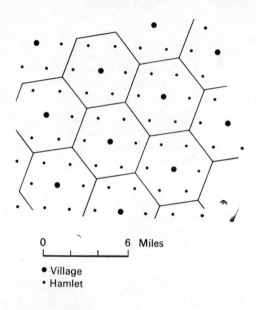

0   6 Miles

● Village
• Hamlet

Fig. 68 Hamlets, villages and towns
in a 'fixed *k*' hierarchy where
k = 4 (Christaller's traffic principle)

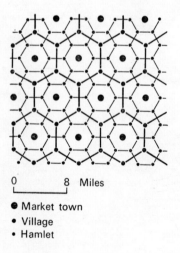

0   8 Miles

● Market town
• Village
• Hamlet

$k = 7$ lattice. In this latter case it can be seen that no settlements are shared between service areas.

Christaller suggested that in theory once a k value had developed within an area it would apply to all the levels in the hierarchy so formed (see fig. 65 where $k = 3$ at both the village and market town levels). This is Christaller's fixed k hierarchy principle.

Christaller suggested that a fixed k value of 3 would develop where the supply of goods from the central places is to be as near the dependent places as possible. This condition maximises the number of central places in the hypothetical landscape, and is referred to as the marketing principle of Christaller. On the other hand, Christaller suggested that a $k = 4$ system would develop where the cost of constructing transport networks is of importance. Figure 68 shows the $k = 4$ lattice developed to the order of the market town. Here it can be seen that as many important places as possible lie on any one traffic route. This is Christaller's traffic principle.

If firm administrative control were important, then a fixed k system of value 7 would develop. In this case all six dependent places would owe allegiance to the central place only and not have divided loyalties. Figure 69 shows a fixed k system of value 7 developed through to the market town level, under Christaller's administrative principle.

| *Fig. 69* 'Fixed k' hierarchy of $k = 7$
developed to third order of settlement
(market towns) (Christaller's
administrative principle)

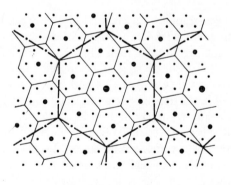

0   10 Miles

● Market town
● Village
· Hamlet

Measure the expected distances for the separation of villages and towns in both cases if the original hamlets in the landscapes with k values of 4 and 7 were at distances of two miles from each other (see figs. 66 and 67). How do these values, and those for the $k = 3$ system compare for the values obtained in the Norwich area in chapter 6?

One of the problems associated with Christaller's fixed k system of values 3 and 4, is that dependent places are divided in their allegiance to the central places one higher in the hierarchy. Christaller recognised this and overcame it by suggesting that what he referred to as 'nesting' would occur. This is explained in fig. 70. In this diagram, it is suggested that in the case of a $k = 3$ hierarchy connections would be set up between two dependent settlements and the central place, and with the $k = 4$ and $k = 7$ hierarchies it is suggested that connections will develop in a similar way in the manner shown.

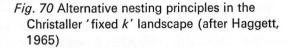

Fig. 70 Alternative nesting principles in the Christaller 'fixed k' landscape (after Haggett, 1965)

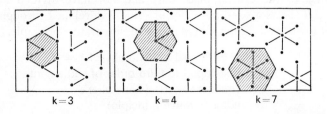

k=3   k=4   k=7

The German geographer, Lösch, in 1954 used the same hexagonal lattices for his theoretical landscape. But he did not consider that a fixed k system approached reality. He took Christaller's model and developed a more sophisticated form by superimposing all the various hexagonal systems so far discussed ($k = 3$, $k = 4$ and $k = 7$) and many more. By superimposing all the lattices on one point, and rotating them he achieved six sectors with many relatively high order settlements, and six sectors which were relatively impoverished of high order settlements (see fig. 71). Under this system of a variable k hierarchy the pattern of settlements produced is much closer to reality. It produces an almost continuous sequence of settlement size, close to the logarithmic distribution found in the Norwich area. This contrasts strongly with the Christaller system which produces settlements in distinct tiers. Not only does this idea apply to population sizes of settlements, but it also refers to the functional content in terms of suppliers of goods and services.

The discussion in this chapter has hinged on the development of centres supplying goods and services, or providing an administrative function. In a developing area, where improved farming techniques are being introduced, surplus food is needed to support the rising urban and service population. Therefore a balanced development is required in those areas which are emerging from a subsistence economy. Britain was going through this stage up to the middle of the eighteenth century, and many agricultural economies of the tropics have reached it in recent decades. However, the theories concerning central place and settlement hierarchies have been grossly distorted in many areas by industrialisation and increasing ease of communications.

Fig. 71 Löschian landscape developed by the rotation of a number of *k*-system hexagons, developing 'city rich' and 'city poor' sectors (after P. Haggett, 1965)
  A. 'City rich' and 'city poor' sectors in Löschian landscape
  B. Distribution of large cities in Löschian landscape
  C. Distribution of all centres in one sector

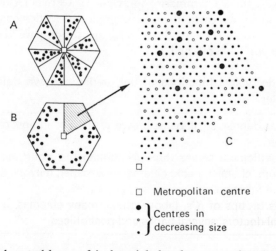

☐   Metropolitan centre

•
○   Centres in decreasing size
•

Ignoring the problems of industrial developments for the moment, it can be seen that any settlement pattern is unlikely to follow closely the theoretical patterns suggested by Christaller, Lösch or any other settlement geographer. Variations in the basic patterns will occur. Many geographers would suggest that the basic pattern of settlement is developed due to such economic laws, and that other factors (e.g. the physical background – distribution of hills and plains, of fertile and infertile soils, of high and low rainfall, etc.), only distort this basic pattern. This implies that to understand the pattern in any area, one must first understand the relevant geographical theory, and then examine the variations from this basic pattern in the light of variations in agricultural potential, relief, etc. Other geographers would disagree with this approach, indicating that each area would have to be examined on its own merit, starting perhaps, with the physical background.

On tracing paper draw Christaller's networks of a k value of 3, 4 and 7 with the distances between the hamlets the same as the average distance between the hamlets in the Thetford area. The scale of the trace should be made the same as that of the map, fig. 31. Try to fit the traces to the hierarchy of settlements seen in the actual areas. What k value trace or combination of values seems to fit the area the best? Comment on the value of theoretical models to the understanding of the settlement pattern and hierarchy of an area.

An interesting example of the fitting of theory to 'reality' can be found in chapter 3 of *The Geography of Market Centers and Retail Distribution*, where B. J. L. Berry analyses the distribution of market centres in a part of Czechwan in central China.

Figures 72 and 73 summarise the views of Christaller on the typical functions to be expected in various grades of settlement and on the spacing and size of these grades of settlement. Compare his conclusions with those you have reached.

Fig. 72 The typical functions of the grades of town detected by W. Christaller

---

M	Doctor, dentist, small bank, brewery, mills, head post office, railway station
A	This settlement serves three *M* settlements, court, library, school, museum, chemist, bank, cinema, newspaper, railway, special shops
K	Capital function
B	Serves groups of *K*'s, labour office, many cinemas, a daily paper, special doctors, several banks and post offices

---

Less is said about the *G*, *P* and *L* settlements except that examples of *L* are given – Munich, Frankfurt, Stuttgart and Zürich. Christaller recognises two further grades of settlement, which are listed in fig. 52, the Reichsteile (Hamburg, Köln, Essen) and the Reichstadt (Berlin).

Fig. 73 The status and distribution of towns as based on the theoretical distribution of centralised services (W. Christaller)

Grades of towns		Population	Distance apart in miles	Service areas in square miles
1. Marktort	*M*	1,000	4·5	18
2. Amstort	*A*	2,000	7·5	54
3. Kreistadt	*K*	4,000	13·0	160
4. Bezirkstadt	*B*	10,000	22·5	480
5. Gavstadt	*G*	130,000	39·0	1,500
6. Provinzstadt	*P*	100,000	67·5	4,500
7. Landstadt	*L*	500,000	116·0	13,000

Read

BERRY, B. J. L. and PRED, A. 'Walter Christaller's *Die Zentralen Orte in Suddeutschland*—Abstract of Theoretical Parts' in *Readings in Economic Geography—The Location of Economic Activity*, pp. 65–68.

BERRY, B. J. L. *Geography of Market Centers and Retail Distribution.*

BUNGE, W. *Theoretical Geography*, chapter 6, particularly pp. 133–51.

CHORLEY, R. J. and HAGGETT, P. *Socio-Economic Models in Geography*, Methuen, 1968, esp. Chapter 9 pp. 303–360 on *Models of Urban Geography and Settlement Location* by B. J. Garner.

DICKINSON, R. E. *The City Region in Western Europe*, pp. 32–40.

HAGGETT, P. *Locational Analysis in Human Geography*, pp. 48–55 and 118–25.

VALAVANUS, A. 'Lösch on Location' in *Readings in Economic Geography—The Location of Economic Activity*, pp. 69–74.

Further reading

CHRISTALLER, W. (1933) *Central Places in Southern Germany*, trans. C. W. Baskin. Prentice-Hall, 1966, esp. Part IB, pp. 27–83, Part II, pp. 137–68.

10 Settlement growth
and decline

Settlements change in size and form in constant, though usually delayed, response to the changing economic and social development of the surrounding areas. Throughout Britain some settlements have grown very rapidly while others have declined just as quickly. Figure 32 (p. 46) shows the population figures for 1921 and 1961 for the settlements in the Norwich area. Also shown is the percentage change for each settlement between these dates. The average rate of population growth for the United Kingdom over this period was 21·1 per cent. In East Anglia, the average rate of growth was 14·2 per cent. Can you explain the difference between these two figures? Would you expect to find a different rate of growth in the Norwich area between 1961 and 1968?

A simple view of the growth and decline of the settlements can be seen by plotting the rates of change on tracing paper superimposed on the map of the Norwich area (fig. 31, facing page 45). A definite pattern can be seen, and many factors could be considered in attempting to explain this pattern, but the following may help to explain the distribution:

1. The size or order of settlements, i.e. have any classes of settlement a population growth or decline greater or smaller than other classes?

2. The proximity of individual settlements to 'A' roads.

3. The proximity of individual settlements to railway stations.

4. The number and type of industries present in any settlement.

5. The proximity of a larger settlement.

Using the ideas suggested in 1 to 5 above, attempt to explain the population changes seen in the area. Graphs and diagrams should be presented as evidence to explain your views.

The following exercises are included for those who require some guidance in their work. They can be allocated to various groups within the class or done by individual students.

a. Calculate the average growth for each of the class-groups of settlement (hamlet, village, town and city). Do any of these averages exceed the national or regional average?

b. Divide the percentage change of population figures into 10 per cent groups, ranging from −40 per cent to +150 per cent. This will give nineteen classes. These nineteen classes should be used as the *x*-axis of a graph with the *y*-axis showing the frequency of occurrences which fall into each of the 10 per cent classes (see fig. 74). After calculating the

Fig. 74 Construction of histogram to show a number of settlements within selected limits of growth or decline

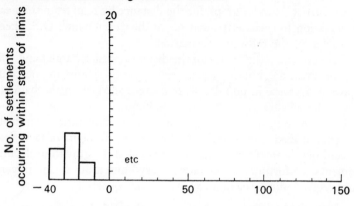

Percent increase or decrease 1921 - 1961

frequency within each 10 per cent class a bar-graph or histogram can be constructed. Comment on the form of the histogram you have drawn.

c. Compare the number of settlements which show a population increase of over 20 per cent (the national average) with the number of settlements that show an increase less than the national average or an actual decline. What does this information suggest about the area?

d. Using the form of graph shown in fig. 75, plot the distance from the nearest 'A' road for each settlement as the y-axis against its percentage increase or decrease between 1921 and 1961. Hamlets should be

Fig. 75 Construction of a graph to show relationship between settlement type and their percent increase or decrease in population 1921–61, and distance from nearest A road

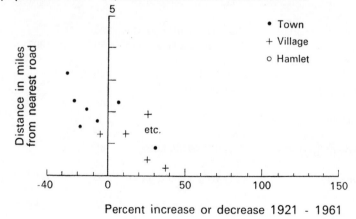

Percent increase or decrease 1921 - 1961

plotted as small open circles, villages as small crosses, and towns as large dots.

e. Construct a similar graph for the distance by road from the nearest railway station to each settlement using the quarter-inch O.S. sheet of East Anglia for the railway information.

f. Using the map (fig. 31), plot the distance of each hamlet and village from its nearest neighbouring town as the *y*-axis against the percentage increase or decrease in population as in fig. 75. Mark in the hamlets as dots and the villages as small crosses as before.

g. Using the information given by fig. 76, the distribution of industries in this part of East Anglia, try to find out if the numbers of factories, or the recent development of industry has affected the growth or decline of settlements. Unfortunately the data is very limited but it can, in certain examples give indications of an answer to this question.

As a very general conclusion what can now be said about the distribution of those settlements showing an increase of population and those showing a decrease ? What does this suggest about the changes in dwelling habits of the people in Britain during this period ? What is the sociological background of these changes in the distribution of population ? Do you think this trend will continue ?

Fig. 76 Industries in the Norwich area

Number and type of industry	Name of the company	Number of people employed	Date of company's formation
Attleborough			
1 Cider	William Gaymer and Sons Ltd.	246	1843
East Dereham			
1 Trailers, transporters	Crane Fruehauf Trailers Ltd.	600	
2 Sugar Beet knives	Dreibholz and Floering Ltd.	60	1907
3 Engineering, saws, fretwork	Hobbies Ltd.	160	
4 Furniture	Jentique Ltd.	340	
5 Clocks	Metamec Ltd.	400	
6 Wood, Building Construction	Potter Bros.	200	
7 Transport Services	F. and G. Smith Ltd.	65	
8 Maltster	A. G. Rix	65	
9 Engineering	J. J. Wright and Sons Ltd.	225	1887
Diss			
1	Aldrich Brothers Ltd.	150	1956

Number and type of industry	Name of the company	Number of people employed	Date of company's formation
2 Resistors, relay devices	Alma Components Ltd.	150	1955
3 Capacitors	Alston Capacitors Ltd.	–	1955
4 Haulage transport	Batrum's Road Services Ltd.	80	
5 Clothing	Richard Emms Ltd.	250	
6 Machinery	K. and C. Moulding (England) Ltd.	20	
7 Paper pulp board	Thompson and Foster (Containers) Ltd.	100	
8 Food	Waveney Valley Packers (Diss) Ltd.	170	
Downham Market			
1 Grain Mill	F. Bird Downham Mills Ltd.	–	
2 Engineering	Downham Engineering Co. Ltd.	75	
3 Rubber, plastics	Choodler Ltd.	34	
4 Plastics	Kenneth Forbes (Plastics) Ltd.	30	
5 –	Favor Parker Ltd.	150	
Brandon			
1 Wood buildings	Green Brothers (Brandon) Ltd.	150	
2 Wood buildings	Lightweight Panels (East Anglia) Ltd.	–	
3 Non-metallic minerals	Lignacite (Brandon) Ltd.	–	
4 Leather, furs	Sand Plingwoods Ltd.	60	
5 Leather, furs	W. Rought Ltd.	100	
6 Wood heels, building	W. Toleman and Son Ltd.	100	
7 Steel, Aluminium stock	Miles Druce Services Ltd.	150	
8 Ladies', Children's Clothes	Miln, Cartwright and Reynolds Ltd.	200	1928
Newmarket			
1 Electrical, electronics	H. and B. Benson Ltd.	15	
2 Caravans, transport	Caravans International Ltd.	2,000	
3 Transport	Eccles Caravans Ltd.	140	
4 Shoes, clothes, leather	F. Gibson (Saddlers) Ltd.	25	
5 Building contractors	H. Holland Ltd.	75	
6 Relays, timers, circuits	Magnetic Devices Ltd. (Pye)	700	1948
7 Transistors	Newmarket Transistors Ltd. (Pye)	400	
8 Machinery	Sprite Ltd.	600	
9 Machinery, equipment	Ernest A. Webb Ltd.	120	

Number and type of industry	Name of the company	Number of people employed	Date of company's formation
Stowmarket			
1 Transport	O. Barnard and Sons Ltd.	130	
2 Factory paints	ICI Paint Division	–	
3 Beverages, chemicals	Munton and Fison Ltd.	120	
4 Wood products	T. Sampson Ltd.	–	
5 Boards	Stramit Boards	–	
6 Metals, machinery	Suffolk Iron Foundry (1920) Ltd.	850	1920
7 Leather, tannery	Webb and Sons (Combs) Ltd.	70	
Eye			
1 Boards	Stramit Boards	–	1945
Swaffham			
1 Chemists, dental specialists	W. E. Powell and Co. Ltd.	15	
2 Furniture, fittings	I.R.S. Ltd.	35	
3 Building construction	Walter Lawrence (East Anglia) Ltd.	–	
Thetford			
1 Rubber, plastics	Baxter Laboratories Ltd.	250	
2 Chemicals, plastics	Breckland Plastics Ltd.	–	
3 Oil burners, steam boilers	British Oil Burners Ltd.	60	
4 Music plates	Caligraving Ltd.	20	
5 Machinery, equipment	J. A. Clarke and Co. (Engineers) Ltd.	36	
6 Refrigerators	Clarke-Built (Williams) Ltd.	50	1947
7 Thermometers	The Electrical Thermometer Co. Ltd.	30	1952
8 Metals	Instruments Machining Services Ltd.	25	
9 Electrical, electronics	Mole Richardson (England) Ltd.	254	
10 Machinery	Rayham Developments	–	
11 Hydraulic lifts	Sheppard Fabrications	100	
12 Welding, cutting equipment	Sheppard Fabrications	–	
13 Thermos	Thermos Ltd.	–	
14 Plastics	Thetford Moulded Products Ltd.	80	
15 Steel fabrication	E. Thornton Engineering Co. Ltd.	–	1962
16 Hardware	20th Century Hardware Ltd.	60	

Number and type of industry	Name of the company	Number of people employed	Date of company's formation
17 Filters	U.C.C. Filters Ltd.	70	
18 Plastic films	Vacuum Research Ltd.	–	
19 Storage	Williams Cold Storage (Thetford) Ltd.	30	
Bury St Edmunds			
1 Pocket spring balances	Abbey Manufacturing Co. (Suffolk) Ltd.	15	
2 Switches, valves	Almot Controls Ltd.	35	1934
3 Malting	Associated British Maltsters	–	
4 Roadmaking machinery	Barber-Greene, Olding and Co. Ltd.	375	1945
5 Transport machinery	The Catchpole Engineering Co. Ltd.	150	
6 Beverages	J. Gough and Sons Ltd.	26	
7 Brewing	Greene, King and Sons Ltd.	750	
8 Harvesters, balers	J. Mann and Sons Ltd. (Suffolk)	120	1947
9 Tools, jigs, dies, moulds	Precision Engineering Products (Suffolk) Ltd.	100	1947
10 Food, bacon	St. Edmund's Bacon Factory Ltd.	290	
11 Flooring	S. and S. Flooring Services Ltd.	35	
12 Civil Engineers	Thomas Stewart (Contractors) Ltd.	400	1946
13 Confectionery	Van Mella Ltd.	100	1900
14 Engineering	W. Vintern Ltd.	–	
15 Distributive	Chas. R. Watson and Co. Ltd.	80	
16 Non-metal minerals	Henry Watson's Pottery Ltd.	25	
17 Poultry Processing	E. B. Packers and Distributors Ltd.	50	1922
18 Bulbs	Vitality Bulbs Ltd.	–	
19 Electronics	T. W. Electronics	6	
20 Timber	Whitmores Timber Co. (1918) Ltd.	25	1918
Norwich			
1 Shoes, clothing	Andrews Heels Ltd.	–	
2 Business	Anglia Television Ltd.	400	
3 Non-metal minerals	Anglian Building Products Ltd.	500	

Number and type of industry	Name of the company	Number of people employed	Date of company's formation
4 Transport equipment	Arterial Motor Bodies Ltd.	100	
5 Mining	Atlas Sand and Gravel Ltd.	200	
6 Business machinery	Auto-Wrappers (Norwich) Ltd.	200	
7 Mining, building construction	Baker and Pointer	45	
8 Machinery, equipment	Balding Engineering Ltd.	350	
9 Fashion Shoes	Bally's Shoe Factories (Norwich) Ltd.	1,400	
10 Metal goods	Barnards Ltd.	380	
11 Metal goods, machinery	Barnes and Pye Ltd.	115	
12 Tinplate containers	J. Billig and Son Ltd.	450	1930
13 Distribution	W. J. Boddy and Sons Ltd.	52	
14 Adding machines	Burroughs Machines Ltd.	–	
15 Building, non-metal minerals	Bush Builders (Norwich) Ltd.	250	
16 Public relation consultants	Business Information Ltd.	–	
17 Scientific instruments	Caley Crackers Ltd.	350	
18 Building civil engineers	R. G. Carter Ltd.	1,800	1921
19 Holding Company	Clover Industries Ltd.	900	
20 Tonic wine, food, drink	Coleman and Co. Ltd.	210	
21 Food, drink	J. J. Colman Ltd.	1,300	
22 Shoes, clothing	Cook's (Norwich) Ltd.	–	
23 Machinery	E. Cowles (Norwich) Ltd.	50	
24 Advertising agents	Crickmay Barnes Ltd.	8	
25 Thermostats, switches, relays	Diamond H. Controls Ltd.	600	1896
26 Banking, insurance, finance	Norman Dixon Ltd.	–	
27 Distributive	East Anglian Trading Co.	20	
28 Newspaper	Eastern Counties News-paper Ltd.	600	
29 Shoes, clothing	Edwards and Holmes Ltd.	700	
30 Machinery	E. R. A. Electronics Ltd.	12	
31 Warehouses	P. F. Fitzmaurice	50	1919
32 Printing, publishing	Fletcher and Sons Ltd.	130	
33 Shoes	Florida Shoe Factory (Norwich) Ltd.	400	
34 Toothpaste	Gordon-Moore Ltd.	–	
35 Fibreboard containers	F. Gough Ltd.	140	
36 Containers	Gough Packaging Ltd.	140	1933

Number and type of industry	Name of the company	Number of people employed	Date of company's formation
37 Engineering	Harford Engineering Co. Ltd.	–	
38 Shoes, clothing	F. W. Harmer and Co. Ltd.	750	
39 Electrical engineering	Heatrae Ltd.	500	
40 Building contractors	Hey Hoe Bros (Norwich) Ltd.	100	
41 Shop fittings	Holmes (Norwich) Ltd.	100	
42 Metal products	Hopper Engineering Ltd.	140	
43 Shoes, clothing	Arthur Howlett Ltd.	200	
44 Ironwork, machinery	Hubbard Bros. Ltd.	65	
45 Axle gears, vehicles	A. W. Hunton and Co. Ltd.	100	
46 Mining, non-metal minerals	Hydraulic Precasts Ltd.	65	
47 Printers	Jarrold and Sons Ltd.	1,000	1770
48 Foundry	L. C. Jay and Sons Ltd.	50	1925
49 Foundry	Jeckells and Sons Ltd.	140	
50 Boxes, plywood	Jewson and Sons Ltd.	1,400	1836
51 Metals, demolition plant	A. King and Sons Ltd.	450	1898
52 Chocolates, sweets	J. Mackintosh and Sons Ltd.	2,500	
53 Electrical engineers	Lawrence, Scott and Electromotors Ltd.	4,500	1883
54 Plastic and leather handbags	D. Maclaren Ltd.	200	1944
55 General engineering	Mann Egerton and Co. Ltd.	2,700	
56 Printers, boxes	Mansfields (Norwich) Ltd.	200	
57 Caravans	Marston Caravans Ltd.	70	
58 Food	Bernard Matthews Ltd.	350	
59 Factory	May and Baker Ltd.	–	
60 Signs	Perpex Ltd.	–	1959
61 Electric organs	Miller Organs Ltd.	50	
62 Shoes	Norvic Shoe Company Ltd.	4,000	
63 Vehicle bodies	Norwich Coachworks Ltd.	50	
64 Factory	Norwich Manufacturing Co. Ltd.	–	
65 Building society	Norwich Union Fire Insurance Society Ltd.	–	
66 Printing	Page Bros. Ltd.	200	
67 Metal products	A. E. Plumstead and Son Ltd.	–	

Number and type of industry	Name of the company	Number of people employed	Date of company's formation
68 Non-metal minerals	Harry Pointer (Norwich) Ltd.	–	
69 Building, distributive	Harry Pointer (Norwich) Ltd.	450	
70 Transport	Pointer's Transport Ltd.	250	
71 Transport, building	Pointer's Tanker Service	65	
72 Building	Readicrete Ltd.	100	
73 Non metals, machinery	E. G. Reeve and Sons Ltd.	30	
74 Footwear, metals	Regency Covers Ltd.	140	
75 Shoes	R. Roberts (Norwich) Ltd.	120	
76 Shoes	P. Segger (Norwich) Ltd.	50	
77 Shoes	Sexton Son and Everard Ltd.	1000	
78 Shoes	Shorton and Armes Ltd.	160	
79 Scientific Instruments	Tom Smith Ltd.	350	
80 Civil engineering	Sir Frederick Snow and Partners	340	
81 Shoes	James Southall and Co. Ltd.	780	
82 Building	Robert Stevenson Ltd.	300	
83 Wood, distributive	A. R. Taylor Co. Ltd.	130	
84 Rubber, plastics	H. Thompson and Sons Ltd.	–	
85 Mining, building	Thomas Gravel Pits Ltd.	65	
86 Plastic containers	U. G. Key Plastics Ltd.	–	
87 Shoes	Van Dal Shoes Ltd.	400	
88 Chemicals	Westwick Distributors Ltd.	–	
89 Food	White Cottell and Co. Ltd.	–	
90 Transport	Windboats Ltd.	66	
91 Television advertising	W.T.V. Studios Ltd.	4	
92 Gravel	Wivenhoe Sands, Stone and Gravel Co. Ltd.	36	
Wymondham			
1 Brushes	Briton Brush Co Ltd.	450	1746
Kings Lynn			
1 Sand quarry	Joseph Boam Ltd.	–	
2 Soups	Campbell's Soups Ltd.	900	
3 Bearings	Cooper Roller Bearings Co. Ltd.	800	1907
4 Boilers, canning machinery	Alfred Dodman Co. Ltd.	100	
5 Food	Dornay Foods	400	

Number and type of industry	Name of the company	Number of people employed	Date of company's formation
6 Chemicals	Dow Chemicals (UK) Ltd.	–	
7 Transport services	Garland and Flexman	16	
8 Filter papers	J. J.'s (Chromatography) Ltd.	20	1958
9 Cement, cement paints	Kerner-Greenwood and Co. Ltd.	–	1910
10 Chemicals, machinery	E. C. Longmate Ltd.	75	
11 Wall panelling	Panawall Co. Ltd.	–	
12 Phones	Pattrick and Thompsons Ltd.	100	
13 Storage	Pointer Storage Ltd.	35	
14 Engineering, casting	Savages Ltd.	52	1850
15 Transport, storage	J. T. Stanton and Co. Ltd.	150	1898
16 Transport, storage	Sommerfeld and Thomas (King's Lynn) Ltd.	–	
17 Vending machines	Stockdales Industrial Venders Ltd.	75	
18 Waterproofing	Universal Building Waterproofers Ltd.	–	
19 Chemicals fertilisers	W. Norfolk Fertilisers Ltd. (Fisons)	–	1872
20 Transport	Garland and Flexman	16	
21 Distributive	Peatling and Cawdron Ltd.	–	
22 Cartons, boxes	Horace Slade and Co. Ltd.	70	1775

Source: Kompass United Kingdom 1967

Read

The South East Study. H.M.S.O. for Ministry of Housing and Local Government, 1964.

CHISHOLM, M. (1964), 'Must we all live in the South East?' *Geography*, vol. 49, 1964.

South East England, White Paper, H.M.S.O., 1964.

Complete Atlas of the British Isles, Reader's Digest, pp. 114–16.

DURY, G. H. *British Isles: Systematic and Regional Geography*, Heinemann Educational, 1964, Chapter 24.

MITCHELL, J. B., ed. *Great Britain, Geographical Essays*, Cambridge University Press, 1962, chapters 3, 5.

OGILVIE, A. G., ed. *Great Britain*, 2nd edn. Cambridge University Press, 1937, chapter 7.

11 Movement between settlements

In chapter 10 the effect of proximity of smaller to larger settlements was shown to be an important factor in the growth of the former. This, of course, is not the only factor but it does seem that the growth of groups of settlements is favoured both by their size relative to others, and by their proximity and their accessibility to each other.

Fig. 77 Portion of British Rail timetable between Catford Bridge and Charing Cross or Cannon Street

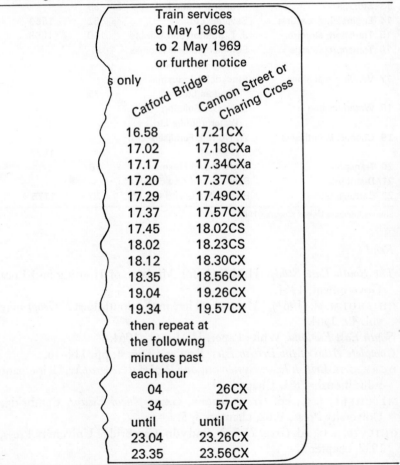

Train services
6 May 1968
to 2 May 1969
or further notice

s only

Catford Bridge

Cannon Street or Charing Cross

Catford Bridge	Cannon Street or Charing Cross
16.58	17.21CX
17.02	17.18CXa
17.17	17.34CXa
17.20	17.37CX
17.29	17.49CX
17.37	17.57CX
17.45	18.02CS
18.02	18.23CS
18.12	18.30CX
18.35	18.56CX
19.04	19.26CX
19.34	19.57CX

then repeat at
the following
minutes past
each hour

04	26CX
34	57CX

until

23.04	23.26CX
23.35	23.56CX

It can be shown that 'distance' as a concept is not as simple as it might first appear. The answers which might be given to a lost traveller's question, 'How far is it to ... ?' indicate this. For example, 'It's about twenty-five minutes to Catford Bridge', or 'It's a fourpenny bus ride to Wembley Park', shows that distance need not be considered only in terms of miles.

The distance between Catford Bridge and Charing Cross is seven and a half miles. Figure 77 shows a section of the British Rail timetable service between these two stations at the beginning of 1968. As can be seen the 'time–distance' varies between sixteen and twenty-five minutes, whereas the 'cost–distance' remains at 2s 3d.

Is it more realistic to visualise the distance between Catford Bridge and Charing Cross in terms of miles (by rail) or time (by rail)? How realistic are either of these distances to a car driver held up by the rush-hour traffic on the South Circular Road outside Catford Bridge Station, or to a schoolboy who finds he has only 1s 6d for the 2s 3d fare to go up to town for an organ lesson after school?

If ideas of distance can vary in this manner, so too can ideas of shape of parts of the earth's surface. Remember that this will also depend greatly upon the location of the viewer.

Look at fig. 78, this shows an easily recognisable map of Britain – as it might be seen by a viewer in a satellite. Such a map, found in most atlases, is very familiar. On it is marked the main British Rail network (with some additional lines), and a number of towns served by British Rail.

Examination of the map would suggest that Milford Haven and Holyhead are about the same distance from London. This is certainly true in terms of mileage or cost (which here is related directly to mileage). But is this realistic from the point of view of a rail traveller in London?

Look at fig. 79 which shows the twenty-seven towns marked on fig. 78, with the distance of each by rail from London. Also for each town is its compass bearing from London, the cost of the second class single fare (1905 and 1968), and the time, in minutes, of the fastest train from London for both 1910 and 1968.

For the potential rail traveller in London (with adequate money) it would be interesting to construct a map of Britain as it appears in terms of time–distance. Figure 80 indicates how this may be done using a scale of one inch to represent 200 minutes travelling time (a larger scale may be used with effect if space permits). First select a point towards the bottom righthand corner to represent London, then draw two axes at right-angles to each other through London representing north–south and east–west. Using a compass draw circles centred on London at half

Fig. 78 British Rail main network

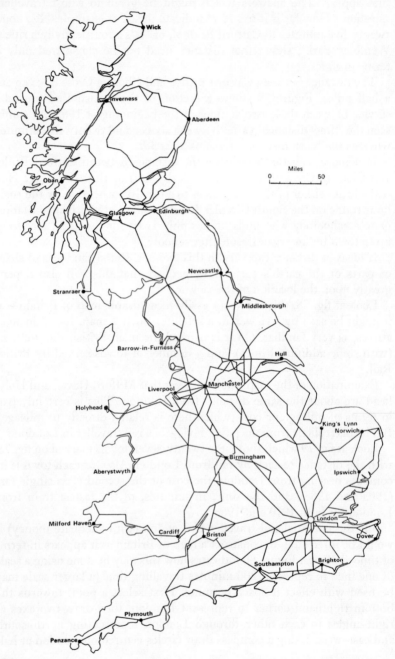

Fig. 79 Details of mileages, directions, fares and times of trains from London to selected towns in Britain for 1905/1910 and 1968

Town	Miles from London	Bearing in degrees from London	Single fare in shillings 1905		Single fare in shillings 1968		Fastest train time taken in mins 1910	Fastest train time taken in mins 1968
			s	d	s	d		
Aberdeen	523½	349	40	0	126	0	630	600
Aberystwyth	234¼	291	19	8½	64	0	425	228
Barrow	264¾	325	22	0½	71	0	370	304
Birmingham	110½	312	9	5	30	6	120	90
Brighton	50½	182	4	2½	14	0	60	55
Bristol	118¼	270	9	9½	32	0	120	110
Cardiff	145¼	270	12	9	39	9	172	132
Dover	77¼	111	6	5½	21	3	105	90
Edinburgh	393	339	32	8	95	0	470	350
Glasgow	401¼	325	33	0	101	0	475	440
Holyhead	263¾	304	22	0	71	0	315	275
Hull	196¾	356	14	0	53	6	370	195
Inverness	568	340	42	6	128	0	815	715
Ipswich	68¾	051	5	9	18	9	90	72
Kings Lynn	97	013	*		26	6	151	127
Liverpool	193¾	318	16	6	52	9	170	155
Manchester	183½	328	15	5½	50	0	215	150
Middlesbrough	238¾	348	19	10½	64	0	330	219
Milford Haven	259½	275	*		70	0	405	381
Newcastle	268½	346	22	7½	72	0	318	230
Norwich	115	036	9	5½	31	3	155	120
Oban	503¾	329	40	11	122	0	895	716
Penzance	305¼	249	25	3	80	0	395	390
Plymouth	225¾	247	18	8	61	0	247	240
Southampton	79¼	234	6	6	21	9	102	70
Stranraer	451½	320	27	6	111	0	572	565
Wick	729½	347	53	3	169	0	1190	1125

Sources: various British Rail publications, *Bradshaw's April 1910 Railway Guide,* David and Charles, 1968
* These lines had not been completed in 1905.

inch, one inch, one and a half inch radii up to seven inches if the compass will allow. Actually, the omission of circles after about five inches is not critical. Each half inch therefore represents a time–distance of 100 minutes from London. Using a protractor it is convenient to mark in (lightly) the angular distances from London at five degree intervals from 0° to 360° (see fig. 79). By using the correct bearing and time–distances from London (fig. 78) plot in the location of the twenty-seven towns.

With some reference to an atlas map, draw in what is now an apparently distorted coastline. The resulting map is quite startling and is a reasonable portrayal of the map of Britain as it appears to the rail traveller in London. There are, of course, many inaccuracies including the fact that only twenty-seven points were chosen; an even more realistic map could be produced based on railway time–distance combined with other forms of transport. This was further developed in an interesting article by Professor Peter Hall, 'Britain's uneven shrinkage', in *New Society*, 14 April 1966.

The map drawn may be considered a distortion of reality, but is it? It could be said that the more usual map of Britain (fig. 78) is just as much a distortion of reality to the rail traveller in London. Such map reconstruction is referred to by geographers as 'topological transformation'.

Fig. 80 Preparation of grid for time-distance transformation of map of Britain (drawn here at half suggested scale)

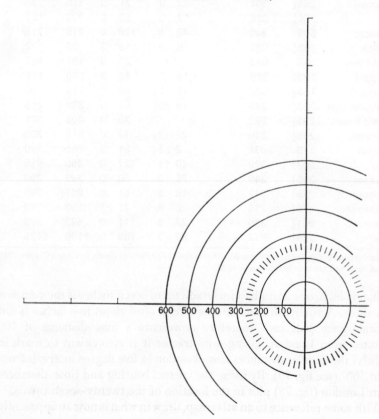

600 500 400 300 200 100

Fig. 81 A British Rail topographical transformation of the map of England between London and Liverpool (the poster in this form appeared in many daily papers in March 1967 after the completion of electrification to Birmingham)

Now you are closer to the heart of England

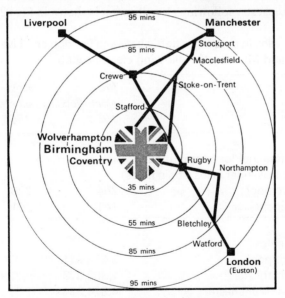

Electrification brings Birmingham a mere 95 minutes from London, Manchester and Liverpool.

Returning now to the comments at the beginning of this chapter concerning the concept of 'nearness' and the effect of proximity and accessibility on neighbouring settlements, it is interesting to look at the transformed spatial characteristics of towns in Britain. Examine the map transformation you have produced. Certain areas or axes appear to have contracted relative to other parts of Britain. What do you think is the significance of the apparently much greater proximity of Liverpool to Manchester, and Birmingham to London? To a lesser extent Bristol and Southampton have also been favoured. How significant will this differential in accessibility become with the opening of the Channel Tunnel? Consider this problem from the point of view of a manufacturer wishing to set up a new factory to supply goods for both a home and an export market. Remember that in many 'growth' industries producer–consumer contact is very important. Does this suggest that certain areas may be specially favoured for future growth?

The extent to which the London–Midlands–Manchester axis has become more favoured in terms of accessibility in recent years may be shown by constructing a similar map transformation for 1910 (see fig. 79). What changes have taken place over this period? This continual process of change is well illustrated by the British Rail poster shown in fig. 81. The extent of the increase in rail passengers between London and Liverpool to Manchester following electrification is shown in fig. 82. Here the

Fig. 82 Increase in passenger traffic between London and Liverpool, and London and Manchester following electrification

	Pre-electrification 1964	Post-electrification 1966
(a)		
Average passenger load throughout journey (passenger miles ÷ train miles)		
Euston–Liverpool	204	226
Euston–Manchester	141	201
(b)		
Passenger miles		
Euston–Liverpool	3,558,041	5,070,504
Euston–Manchester	1,352,373	5,729,383
*St Pancras–Manchester	4,824,234	1,353,900

* The steep rise in passenger miles on the Euston–Manchester route in 1966 was partially due to a transfer of services from the St Pancras–Manchester route

Source: information supplied by British Rail

friction of distance has decreased, and the interaction between the population centres has increased.

This chapter has so far only dealt with rail times, but cost–distances could also be examined, and it must be remembered in many cases that road transport is more important. However road and rail are often in direct competition, and with the introduction of British Rail liner trains significant changes may be expected, despite the opening of further motorways.

Theoretically it would be possible to construct a transformed map of Britain using road times from London, but the obtaining of data would be difficult and costly. Reference to fig. 83 showing the expected pattern of motorways for the early 1970s would suggest that again the Manchester to London axis will be specially favoured.

The significance of changing space relations in terms of time or cost has been referred to before in chapter 3, where this was examined in terms of changes in 'friction of distance'. The development of an efficient and speedy structure of communications, with a resulting decrease in the friction of distance is of vital importance in the development of a region. Differential changes in the friction of distance are likely to favour certain regions perhaps to the detriment of others. It is interesting to consider to what extent this is true of the British Isles, or even on a much larger worldwide scale.

Further work can be carried out, either singly or in groups, using similar techniques. As stated earlier, the location of the viewpoint is important. So far only London has been used, but British Rail timetables will give an indication of the friction of distance to be encountered from centres such as Birmingham, Manchester, Glasgow and Plymouth. If a number of such map transformations were constructed, comparison would indicate the most obviously accessible parts of Britain. Which are these?

In addition to this, studies of your own local area could be carried out to indicate the relative accessibility of certain villages or towns, or parts of the towns in which you live. The construction of map transformations according to cost, time, and using various combinations of transport could reveal some interesting geographical relationships. Further work concerning such map transformations will be dealt with in the book on urban geography.

If polar co-ordinate graph paper is available the drawing of such transformations is relatively simple. Such paper should have concentric circles every tenth of an inch and radial lines every degree (every five or ten degrees thickened). The scale area should be about ten inches by seven inches. If used with an overlay of tracing paper the polar coordinate sheets can be used indefinitely.

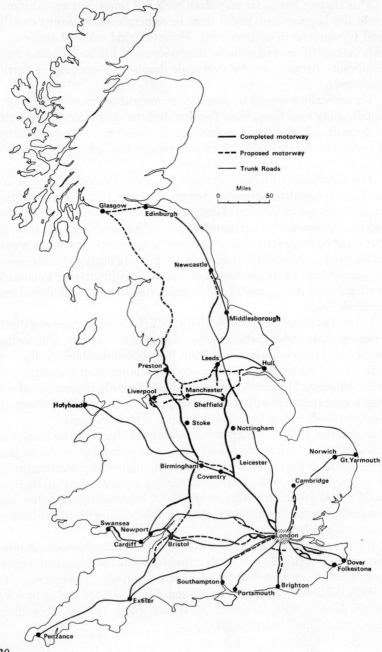

Fig. 83 Proposed motorway network for the early 1970s.
Full detail is not given for Scotland.

Completed motorway

Proposed motorway

Trunk Roads

Miles
0   50

Glasgow
Edinburgh
Newcastle
Middlesborough
Leeds
Preston   Hull
Liverpool   Manchester
Sheffield
Holyhead
Stoke
Nottingham
Norwich
Leicester   Gt.Yarmouth
Birmingham   Cambridge
Coventry
Swansea
Newport
Cardiff   Bristol   London
Dover
Folkestone
Southampton   Brighton
Portsmouth
Exeter

Penzance

Sources for further work

A.B.C. Railway Guide, Thomas Skinner & Co. Obtainable monthly, and includes details of train times, frequencies, and fares, together with mileages from London and size of population.

Bradshaw's April 1910 Railway Guide, David and Charles, 1968.

BRITISH RAIL. *Regional Timetables.*

BRITISH RAIL. Timetable booklets, especially useful being the 'Inter City' version.

Local bus service timetables.

Read

HALL, P. 'Britain's Uneven Shrinkage', in *New Society*, 14 April, 1966.

Further reading

BUNGE, W. 'Distance, Nearness and Geometry', in *Theoretical Geography*, 2nd edn. Lund Studies in Geography, Ser. C, No. 1, 1966.

Selected book list

ALEXANDER, J. W. *Economic Geography*, Prentice-Hall, 1963.

BERRY, B. J. L., *Geography of Market Centers and Retail Distribution*, Prentice Hall, 1967.

BUNGE, W. *Theoretical Geography*, (2nd Edition) Lund Studies in Geography, Ser. C, No. 1, 1966.

CHISHOLM, M. D. *Rural Settlement and Land Use*, Hutchinson's University Library, 1962.

CHORLEY, R. J., and HAGGETT, P., *Frontiers in Geographical Teaching*, Methuen, 1965.

CHORLEY, R. J., and HAGGETT, P., *Socio-Economic Models in Geography*, Methuen, 1968.

DICKINSON, R. E. *City and Region*, Routledge & Kegan Paul, 1965.

DICKINSON, R. E. *West European City*, Routledge & Kegan Paul, 1951.

DURY, G. H. *Map Interpretation*, Pitman, 1960.

GREGORY, S., *Statistical Methods and the Geographer*, Longmans, 1963.

HAGGETT, P. *Locational Analysis in Human Geography*, E. Arnold, 1965.

HOSKINS, W. G. *Making of the English Landscape*, Hodder & Stoughton, 1955.

HOSKINS, W. G. *Fieldwork in Local History*, Faber, 1967.

JONES, E. *Towns and Cities*, Oxford University Press, 1966.

MAYER, J. and KOHN, C. *Readings in Urban Geography*, University of Chicago Press, 1959.

MITCHELL, J. B. *Historical Geography*, English Universities Press (Teach Yourself Series), 1954.

MORONEY, M. J., *Facts from Figures*, Pelican, 1951.

MURPHY, R. E. *The American City*, McGraw-Hill, 1966.

NORBORG, K. *IGU Symposium in Urban Geography*, Lund, 1962.

SMAILES, A. E. *Geography of Towns*, Hutchinson's University Library, 1953.

SMITH, R. H. T., TAAFFE, E. T., and KING, L. J. (Editors), *Readings in Economic Geography—the Location of Economic Activity*, Rand McNally, 1968.

Scientific American, 'Cities', September, 1965; republished as a paperback. Pelican.

Essay titles

1. Suggest reasons why rural settlement is nucleated in some areas and dispersed in others.

2. Analyse the factors which have led to the growth of certain towns into regional centres.

3. Show how large towns affect the non-industrial land use of surrounding areas.

4. How would you make a field study of the functions of a small town?

5. 'Towns very often grow up where man has to change his means of transport'. Discuss.

6. Why do people live in towns?

7. Defence has been a major factor in the siting of settlements. Discuss.

8. Is function the best basis for a classification of settlements? Illustrate from areas you have studied the functions commonly associated with capital cities.

9. 'Planners should look far into the future.' Amplify this statement.

10. What effect will the Severn road bridge have on the interaction between Bristol and Cardiff?

11. 'The land use and history of an area determines the type of rural settlement.' Discuss this statement.

12. 'The basic pattern of settlement is caused by economic factors, relief only distorts.' Discuss this statement.

13. Discuss, with examples, the factors that influence the siting of settlements.

14. Many settlements are sited on river terraces. Discuss and expand this statement.

15. What effect had the enclosure movement between 1750 and 1850 upon the settlement of the Midlands?

16. Discuss the role of place name evidence in assessing the type and distribution of reclaimed areas in Great Britain.

17. Describe and attempt an explanation of the settlement in a rural area of Great Britain of about thirty square miles.

18. 'The distribution of market gardening in Great Britain does not depend solely on climate and soil.' Discuss.

19. Discuss the significance of minor relief features in the settlement of an area.

20. With reference to any rural area you have studied in detail, show how a knowledge of history is necessary to understand its settlement pattern.

21. How would you carry out a study of a small rural area?

Index